Praise for Steven Pybrum's

Money and Marriage

"Finally a clear and simple guideline to track our cash flow, follow our investments and increase our net worth."

—CHRIS AND DONNA PARAMOURE
successful business owners

"The message is clear; you must begin investing and saving for your financial future year by year. You must begin as soon as possible. I advise my clients to follow the Money and Marriage principles."

—WALT HARASTY
attorney-at-law

"Steven Pybrum has guided our financial planning and tax planning for the last twenty years. He has provided us with invaluable guidance, insight, information and support. He is the kind of professional everyone is looking for."

—NANCY COMBS
homemaker

"I should have started tracking and understanding the stock market and investments very early on in my career. We now understand the importance of these principles."

—JOHN COMBS
corporate vice president

"I was so happy to read these down-to-earth financial planning ideas in one place that I ran out and bought copies of Money and Marriage and sent them to each of my adult children."

—BILL BOGUE
corporate president

Money
and
Marriage
Making It Work Together

A Guide to Smart Money Management
and Harmonious Communications

STEVEN PYBRUM, CPA, MBA

ABUNDANCE PUBLISHING

This publication is designed to provide accurate and authoritative information in regard to the subject matter covered. It is sold with the understanding that the publisher is not engaged in rendering legal, accounting or other professional services. If legal advice, accounting advice, tax advice or other expert assistance is required, the services of a qualified, competent professional person in your geographic area should be sought.

10 9 8 7 6 5 4

ISBN: 978-0-9651277-3-8
Library of Congress Catalog Card Number: 96-083730

Pybrum, Steven M.
  Money and marriage : a guide to smart money management and harmonious communications / Steven Pybrum.
  p. cm. — (Money and marriage ; 1)
  Includes index.
  LCCN: 96-83730
  ISBN 978-0-9651277-3-8
  1. Married people—Finance, Personal. 2. Man-woman relationships. I. Title.
HG179.P93 2024   332.024'0655
                                  QB196-20200

Published in 1996, revised 2004, revised 2023-V3.0

Manufactured in the United States of America

Contents

About the Author

STEVEN PYBRUM has been a radio talk show host and producer of the radio program "Tax Tips." He has appeared in newspapers, magazines and professional journals in articles on financial planning and tax planning tips, especially in his own column, "Business Cents." He is a business consultant, helping to establish and manage many entrepreneurial efforts of client companies that are family-owned businesses. Steve also provides consulting services to Fortune 100 companies. Some of the organizations he has assisted are IBM, McDonald's and Bank of America, as well as the United States Senate.

Steve has been writing about technical information for 24 years. He found that he is quite skilled for example in taking complex tax matters found in the Internal Revenue Code and making them easy to understand. Steve has now applied this skill of taking complex matters and putting them in plain English to marriage preparation and marriage skills. Steve has taught at many colleges and universities in the western United States and is often a guest lecturer for business and finance courses.

Steve offers couples weekend retreats in Santa Barbara, California. These getaway weekends allow couples the quiet time they need to grow more aware of and attached to each other. The principles of money management and communication intimacy are taught in these courses. Steve's passion is making champion net worth builders of his students.

Steve hopes that you enjoy this book and put these sound, guiding principles to work in your own life.

Introduction

One of the most difficult parts of a marriage relationship is to talk with your mate about finances. In fact finance is the "hottest rock" to deal with in a relationship. Statistics tell us one-third of all married couples consider money their number one item of battle. Other marriages have conflict over money, but it is not the main cause of battle. Although uncharted, this would move the figure closer to eighty-five percent of all marriages having ongoing disputes about money. Try to sit down at the kitchen table and have a frank discussion about family finances. It's not easy. *Money and Marriage* will serve as an indispensable household guide that will take you through this process as you can communicate openly, frankly and honestly in your comfort zone with your spouse.

Finances are a large issue in a relationship and are often the matter least discussed. Financial misunderstandings comprise a large percentage of the reasons that spouses divorce. *Money and Marriage* puts the issues out there before you. Read this book and actively discuss with your mate what you glean from the chapters.

This book tells you how and gives you direction in how to achieve financial success and presents some wealth building techniques while identifying the roadblocks to your financial prosperity.

Money and Marriage explains what you must do in a relationship to build financial assets. *Money and Marriage* tells you how to do this in an open and healthy way.

Since the early twenties and before, as people built net worth, it has seemed that the marriage relationship had one wealth builder and one person to hide the family checkbook from. This type of wealth building cannot be considered healthy in the twenty-first century.

It takes no brains or training to spend money. It takes careful thought, education and opportunity to create money. If every household would actually save a percentage of their annual earnings, a little bit every year, there would be a comfortable retirement in store for everyone.

When you are able to openly communicate about family finances, then you will place yourself on track for great financial achievement.

Part of financial achievement has to do with building financial net worth. Sufficient net worth first makes work a "want to," not a "have to." When you are sufficiently prosperous, then you can retire. Retirement creates the challenge to maintain your net worth so you can remain retired. With this book I want to teach you how to "retire in style."

To be financially successful you must become good money managers. *Money and Marriage* will become your guidebook to financial freedom, independence and security.

To make this book an effective tool, each spouse should read it on their own. Better yet, each spouse should have their own copy. Read it and underline the important elements **for creating your household's financial success**. In conducting the research necessary to write *Money and Marriage,* I found it helpful to have men underline in blue and women underline in pink. Pick a method that works for your family unit.

Men and women see the world differently. The priorities, cares and concerns of a man are not the same as the priorities, cares and concerns of a woman. Again, you should each have your own copy of this book.

Men and women have many differences in their outlook. Together, in the warmness of the marriage relationship, oneness, unity and completeness are achieved. *Money and Marriage* will identify some of the man–woman differences necessary to have and maintain a healthy, happy and long-lasting marriage relationship.

Once you both have finished reading and underlining your book, you then need to openly discuss what you discovered that might help bring financial success to your household.

If you are unable to make progress with an open, frank discussion on establishing your goals and financial game plan, you should seek the services of a competent family and marriage counselor in your community. These trained professionals can work wonders through the training they have received.

From the author of *Money and Marriage,* best wishes for financial prosperity in your future. It is my prime desire to help you "retire in style."

Acknowledgments

Many hours of research and writing go into a work of this kind. My friends have wondered why I have not been on the golf course or out playing tennis. They have been very supportive and helpful with comments to insert into this book. Some of the comments were a little too humorous to include.

There has been a dedicated group of professionals, peers and friends who have contributed to this book in reviewing, editing and commenting on methods to get the message across.

I am grateful for the hard, earnest work of my friend Leila Stephens for her comments and contributions. I would like to thank the following people for their effort and encouragement. Reading and discussing the book as couples, they provided feedback that was very helpful: John and Nancy Combs, corporate executive; Jim and Donna Olson, corporate president Mr. and Mrs. Walt Harasty, attorney-at-law; Chris and Donna Paramoure, family business owners; Mr. and Mrs. Eldon Edwards, business broker. I hope this book emerges as a work they will show their children and grandchildren with pride and enthusiasm.

I would also like to thank the many health-care professionals who have contributed to this book. Throughout California, I have consulted with psychologists, marriage and family counselors, psychotherapists and psychiatrists. Their contributions were invaluable and are greatly appreciated.

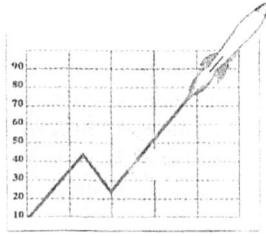

CHAPTER 1

Growing Your Net Worth

What is net worth? At what point is a person considered a millionaire? Is one million enough?

Financial net worth is the result of some basic, third-grade mathematics:

When you have made a list of all your assets and have assigned reasonable market values to them, then you can mathematically arrive at the total of your assets.

Then you need to make a current list of all your debts or liabilities. List everything owed to everyone as of the end of this month. This is the total of your liabilities.

Last, subtract your liabilities from your assets. Congratulations! You have now computed your net worth.

$$\begin{array}{r} \text{Total Financial Assets} \\ -\quad \underline{\text{Total Liabilities}} \\ \underline{\underline{\text{NET WORTH}}} \end{array}$$

Every household in the world should calculate at least annually the household net worth. Each household should maintain a chart showing the trend line growth or erosion of the household net worth. If you chart this annually, you can see pictorially the direction your net worth is growing. A picture speaks a thousand words. This is very true in following the trend of your net worth. If you know and can see that your net worth is not growing as rapidly as you would like, you then can take quicker and more effective action in accelerating its upward growth.

1

Net worth building can be fun and exciting. Instead of shutting your spouse out, include them in the financial planning for your household. Tell your spouse of your ambition and interest in building net worth. Tell your spouse of your plans to increase your net worth each year of your working life. Ask your spouse for their help and support in making this happen.

Not only should you periodically compute net worth, you should complete your family graph and show yourself the upward trend toward building higher net worth each year. Celebrate if you out-perform your goals. Celebrate when you meet your goals. Just plan to celebrate as you build your net worth. Along the way, take all necessary steps to avoid erosion to your net worth.

Know that if you marry someone who is financially irresponsible, it may have been a bad choice on your part, much like making a bad business decision. An irresponsible mate is like inviting a termite over to your lumberyard. Your money is like your woodpile. The termite will make dust of it.

Building net worth requires discipline. Building net worth requires one to keep calm and quiet their impulsive urge to spend. Together formulate ideas of what is good spending and what is wasteful spending.

Participating in a relationship requires you to be consciously aware of some of the ground rules about forming relationships that last. Financial freedom will come much easier if you have a spouse who is financially responsible. Thus, you need to choose a lifetime partner who is aware of and in harmony with your goals to build financial net worth.

Every year as you compute your new net worth, place this computation and picture into a three-ring binder and keep this with your permanent records. Each year add to your binder. Enjoy looking back through the early years of growing your net worth.

Wealth building is a process. You do not have to struggle each year with a budget and try to make ends meet. A better strategy would be finding a source of income that satisfies your need for spending. Most Americans have sufficient earnings to allow waste in their spending habits. Many professionals have created an appearance of artificial wealth, but they are deeply in debt.

You have to gain a sense of wealth building, of how to make your accumulated wealth grow each year. Your wealth grows as you convert some of your career earnings into investments that pay rewards.

If building net worth is important to you, it is essential to have an understanding of the process. Establish habits that will lead you in the direction of increased net worth, and modify those behaviors that do not.

There is no one who is so far in debt that they cannot turn the situation around with some sound financial thinking. Acting quickly will keep your ship from sinking. Everyone can build net worth. Net worth building is for everyone!

You cannot wait until you are older to begin creating wealth. Wealth building is a slow, steady, year-by-year process that takes your talent, ingenuity and attention. You cannot continue to gamble your financial future on future pay raises, bonus monies or winning a lottery. Get a realistic grip on your finances. Make strategies and plans that can help you build something you can look on with pride. Most of all, live within your means. You will need to become focused and directed in managing your money. You need to awaken the desire and enthusiasm to build your wealth into large sums of money.

Working together to build financial net worth allows the couple to define and pursue shared financial goals. These goals can include buying a home, saving for retirement, paying for children's education, or traveling together. Collaborating on these objectives can strengthen their bond and sense of purpose.

Building wealth together can contribute to long-term financial security for both partners, especially in retirement. Joint planning and saving can help ensure that they have the resources needed to enjoy their later years comfortably.

Communication and trust are important parts of working together on financial matters encouraging open communication and trust between partners is a desired result. Discussing financial goals, budgeting, and investment strategies can help you understand each other's priorities and make informed decisions together.

When you get enthusiastically involved in building your net worth, it seems to be magic. As you start to accumulate wealth, new ideas sprout. This creates opportunity for you to convert these new ideas into more wealth. Do not let wealth accumulation frighten you. Do not consider that building wealth is for someone else.

Building wealth is for everyone who wants to awaken that sense within themselves, then put some very basic principles to everyday use. Building wealth can be very fun, exciting and something that will bond you and your spouse together forever. Children are a good bonding agent in a relationship because the parents can stand back and admire what they have created with their physical bodies. When you build wealth, you can admire what you have created with your minds.

You will need to develop strategies and set goals and objectives that work for you and your personal situation. You will need to use your creative powers to plan your financial future. You will need to focus on the direction you have chosen. You will need to apply great effort to get your program and process of wealth building started. Once started, the joy and excitement will propel you into the future. You will become motivated and inspired to grow and build more.

This book provides a lot of direction, we give you the path to get onto to then be able to build your financial net worth. Wealth accumulation is the target and this book gives you a lot of direct guidance in how to do this. Review again this chapter and make a note to stick inside your book in how you mathematically calculate your net worth because net worth building is the underlying topic and theme of this book. Build for your self the net worth building mindset and have your spouse supporting and participating with you in the process. To get there all you have to do is follow the guidance provided in this book.

In the chapters to follow we will investigate why people are afraid to create abundance and wealth. Once you have overcome your fears, you will be available to become builders of abundant wealth. Let's journey together to see how we might all become champion builders of net worth.

MANTRA

I will compute my net worth
at least once per year.

CHAPTER 2

The Marriage Relationship

There are many components to the marriage relationship. The word *relationship* means connection or way of relating. Relationships are all about the connections we have with other people. These connections pave the way for bonding. With bonding you are striving for unity and harmony. This chapter will discuss the components that make up the financial relationship within your marriage.

Choosing the right partner is a very important step in pursuing your goal of building net worth. Mate selection, healthy communications, intimacy and conflict management are skills you will want to master.

If you are reading this and still are in the choosing the right partner stage then read the companion book "Money and Marriage for Engaged Couples." This book goes into detail about how to choose the right partner for you.

Two people in a marriage relationship need to be aware that there is an interpersonal relationship between them. This relationship needs daily watering, management, time, attention and the exchange of information. You have to train each other how to love one another. Tell your partner what makes you feel loved and hope your partner will inform you what makes them feel loved. Then you need to be certain you try to do what makes your partner feel loved. Do not love your partner in the way that makes you feel loved. You will find that this simply will not work. You need to love, adore and appreciate each other on a daily basis in the way each partner feels loved within themselves. Know how you feel loved and express that information in a way that inspires your mate to want to give it to you. Your mate must do the same. Know how your mate experiences love and be willing to give it to them in the way they want it.

At birth, we do not know how to live with others. This is learned behavior. In our daily behavior, knowingly or unknowingly, consciously or unconsciously, we echo the words, reactions and habits we learned from our parents and other adults in our development years. We begin conducting ourselves in our daily adult life using these preprogrammed behaviors. We take these steps and conduct ourselves this way until we become aware there may be a better way. Then we implement change in our daily life. As a couple, this change is necessary to allow for the process of uniting and merging your lives together for a lifetime.

Quickly become aware that you both emerged from different family backgrounds, traditions, customs, methods and socioeconomic strata. In order to merge your lives together, you will have to be open to change. Do not expect that your partner will adopt your ways.

Much like managing your finances, you must both oversee your marriage relationship as if you were managers of something very important to you. Managing requires planning, organizing, setting of goals and objectives, creating a single vision of the future, and a mission or purpose for the union. Managing your relationship requires you to seek and obtain the information, training and coaching necessary to understand the relationship-building process.

Much divorce occurs today because adults did not know they were supposed to communicate during their marriage. Sometimes people are resistant to change during the term of their marriage. Sometimes people do not know how to communicate intimately with one another. All of this could have been avoided with the proper coaching and training on how to conduct oneself in a marriage relationship.

Prior to marriage, you both had your own money and made your own decisions as to how and when it was spent. After you are married, some method of financial pooling is necessary. Early on you must make decisions about how you pool your money and who pays for what. This should be done with the spirit of structuring the greatest possibility for building net worth.

One thing is certain: there are going to be expenses incurred during your relationship. Who, when and how they are paid for needs to be clearly discussed and agreed upon.

To start your financial life within your relationship, you have to make some important structural and financial decisions. You need to discuss how you will take in money and pay out money that comes into your household. You need to arrange your bank accounts so you start out with a financial strategy that helps you build your net worth.

Early in your marriage you need to decide on your accounting method. This format is a matter that should be custom fit to your own needs and individual circumstances. You may simply have a joint account and both spend from this source. Today, however, most successful net worth builders seem to want to have their own separate accounts and contribute to a joint account. This format prevents runaway erosion that can occur when both spouses neglect to watch the one joint account.

There are four generally accepted accounting methods for married couples: the whole wage system (one partner manages all of the money of the household); the allowance system (breadwinner gives the other spouse an allowance to run the household and keeps the rest of the money along with money management responsibilities); the shared management system (both partners have equal access to and responsibility for all family money); and the independent management system (each partner manages a separate income stream exclusively).

You need to pick a method or combination that works best for your household. Select one that causes the least amount of erosion to the resources you are going to invest to grow your net worth.

In the first financial meeting of your marriage relationship, you will want to establish an investment account.

Before a lot of decisions are made, let's review the reasons you might want to build financial net worth. In building financial net worth, you build financial freedom. You will have the income and security you seek to be free from all distractions, and you will be able to participate in, contribute to and enjoy life to the fullest extent. As you build net worth, you will achieve an income level that will allow you to be financially content and happy. As you build, work and use your earnings productively to create more net worth, you will be readying yourself for your retirement years. Simply put, building financial net worth enables you to retire in style.

A cornerstone of building net worth is to sacrifice a little today to get a lot tomorrow. For those of you who have an initial aversion to understanding the net worth building process, the mention of the word sacrifice is enough to make you close this book right now! But in order to build net worth you do not need to sacrifice in the painful sense. All you need to do is manage your money and not let unconscious free spending invade your household the way it has most of the households in this country. A recent study tells us just about 98% of the households in America are financially structured to allow unconscious free spending.

Unconscious free spending is not healthy and should be avoided. With unconscious free spending, you spend years earning money with little to show for your efforts, little or no increase to your financial net worth. Normally, unconscious free spending results in a financial structure that allows the household to incur debt in excess of current earnings. Earnings and expenditures are never viewed together. Many unconscious free spenders are great avoiders of reviewing household expenditures on a monthly basis. Too many families are in hot pursuit of the American dream. Too many families ascribe to the policy of "have credit will travel."

I have heard all of the arguments why net worth building is for someone else. "This is certainly not for our family, we cannot afford it!" Many people say they do not want to save for the future, since they may not live that long. Some people create an image in their own mind that having extra money is somehow evil. The excuses are endless and sometimes very creative.

It is time for American families to wake up. You can no longer put off efforts to build net worth for your family. You must start today. This book will guide you and your loved ones into a healthy and prosperous future. In building your financial future, take those precautions and make those plans that will allow your wealth accumulations to pass on to your children and future generations. Find your reason and purpose in building net worth. Close your eyes and visualize what your life would be like if you allowed wealth creation into your daily life. As a couple, you need to agree that net worth building is something that will be good for your household. The first day of your marriage is not too early to start the process.

Everyone worries that net worth building will cause them to suffer some form of deprivation, such as not being able to do the things they always wanted to do. Yet there are many families out there who have never had combined net annual earnings in excess of $30,000, and they are very happy and content. Money in itself does not bring happiness and contentment. Having money, however, will take away a lot of the financial worry and frustration that accompany having negative net worth.

There are two important points to be made right now.

1. Building net worth can be fun and exciting, and once started you will not feel any sacrifice, deprivation or starvation whatsoever.

2. Building net worth will allow you to have more money and freedom. This will not necessarily bring you happiness and contentment; you must find your own happiness and contentment without relying on money to provide it.

This sounds fine when you read it; everyone could say they would like to be financially successful. I doubt that many readers of this book do not want financial success. But while reading about financial success is easy, achieving financial success for yourself and your family is difficult. Everyone, however, can take steps to annually increase their net worth. Why do so few families actually take these steps for themselves? In life and in your married life sometimes you have to, together reset the compass, which is the direction you are presently going. Reset the compass to get rid of unconscious free spending, wasteful spending and promise to join together to work together to build together your financial net worth, with both partners making a contribution to this important cause.

Let's look at why people of certain age groups don't have a high net worth.

Twenties

Retirement seems so far in the future that not many people in their twenties give more than four hours of conscious thought to retirement during the entire ten-year period. When retirement-minded investments are suggested to them, they often say they cannot even pay for what they have now, retirement is too far off, and they will do that later. Additionally, all earnings are spent on present-day lifestyle.

Thirties

Retirement planning is a nice thought. With attempts to launch a career and the costs of housing and providing for children, not a lot of money seems available to spend on investment or retirement planning products.

Forties

Retirement planning sounds nice and begins to appear on lists of things to do. College tuition payments, recreational toys, material goods and activities prolong the initiation of any positive steps toward investment or retirement planning products.

Fifties

Retirement planning now sounds like something you should be doing. You are beginning to look into what steps to take, which product to buy and what investments to make. College tuition and aging parents are more likely to be the direction of your spending.

Sixties

Wow, I better step up those retirement planning ideas. I will begin to assess what I need to do to make investments that will enable me to have the same income annually that I have become accustomed to spending. I will go seek professional help to find out what investment I must make to enable me to retire at age 65.

You then go to professional investment counselors and financial planners and tell them you have often thought of making some retirement-minded investments, but for various family reasons you have put these investment acquisitions off until now.

You inquire as to how much you must invest and what products will allow you to retire at age 65, providing you with a stream of income to continue your lifestyle as it now exists.

You will find the financial planner or investment counselor is carefully taking notes, trying to understand your needs, goals and objectives. Upon learning you are age 60 and want to begin making investments in products that will enable you to retire at age 65 while maintaining your present level of income, guess what the financial planner or investment counselor is going to tell you?

The financial advisor is going to tell you that your request is impossible! Miracles were not written on the door as you walked in. This goal is impossible to accomplish.

As a financial planner I cannot tell you how many people have wandered into my office repeating this same scenario and looking to me to perform some sort of magic.

Young people should take note and learn from this situation. Do not manage your financial affairs in such a way that you have not provided for your financial freedom at your retirement age.

My favorite technique for awakening young people to retirement-minded investments is to ask an older client into the office on the same day as the younger people, after obtaining the permission of both sides. I invite the older person into the office to tell the younger people what he wished he would have done way back in his twenties. It is impressive to hear both sides. Younger people leave feeling ready to rather aggressively make plans for their financial future.

Most people are financially unable to retire in the style they wish. Recent statistics reveal 95% of the Americans who turn 65 cannot financially afford to retire after a lifetime of work. In almost every case this tragic situation can be traced back to poor planning on the part of these people.

Of the thousands of successful people, I have talked to in creating this book, all of them look back on their financial life and are glad they invested a little bit every year since they were age 25. There is a resounding consensus that it is important to sock a little money away each and every year, increasing the commitment to investment as the years advance.

If you start in your twenties and invest $2,000 annually at the rate of 8% average return on your investment, you will have over $500,000 in cash at age 65.

The hardest part of retirement planning is that all-important first step: getting the investment process started. Once you start, you will be able to watch your investments grow and your net worth soar. The excitement of building a strong financial future will keep the process going. So, regardless of your age right now, you must start the process today.

In order to get the process started, you both must agree to make a commitment to it. You must be solid in your relationship and be able to talk openly about family finances.

The hardest part of discussing family finances is that each person comes to the table with their own agenda. Some of this agenda is because of gender difference. Each person has a list of wants and desires that will use the family finances. Let's look at why talking finances is so hard. Let's look into the makeup of the people who are in the relationship. You must be open to taking a frank look at yourself and where you came from without excuse or denial. It is easy to find fault in a mate, but it is very difficult to look inside of ourselves.

We do not inherently know how to live with others and let them live with us. We all do things out of learned behavior. These are those daily steps we took when we were growing up. Many of the things we do today can be traced back to our childhood. Much of our ability to form relationships stems from our upbringing and our environment during our first 20 years on earth.

You need to nurture and manage your marriage relationship. You cannot sit back and passively accept the fact of your marriage without giving any focused thought to the relationship part of your marriage.

You and your spouse differ as to how you manage money for a number of reasons. First, you are two unique individuals. Second, one spouse is a man, one spouse is a woman. Men and women are different in many ways. The priorities assigned to money are a good way to demonstrate the different man-woman reference points. You have very distinctly different priorities. These man-woman differences have been well researched. You both were brought up in different families of different economic means. Much of the way you deal with money is attached to your childhood upbringing. These attitudes go back to your family's cultural and ethnic makeup, education level, career status and economic background. You have absorbed your parents' feelings about money. Your core beliefs provide very different internal reference points.

Your core beliefs are the software you are running on your mental computer, the subconscious mind. This software has the stored-up habits that you use when a new situation enters your day. Through choice, you can remove the old programs and install new programs that lead you into health, wealth, abundance and prosperity. If your office computer software becomes outdated, don't you elect to change the software? From your core belief structure, you formulate and make decisions about how to earn, handle, utilize, invest and manage money. Know that you and your spouse have very different core beliefs. Over time you may be able to change, abandon, modify and merge your core beliefs into a unified system. Through active communication, you compare notes about your core beliefs, compare notes about your desire to earn money, compare notes about your desire to spend money, compare notes about your desire to invest money, and compare notes on how to make yourselves champion net worth builders. Work toward making an agreement to change your core beliefs and work together toward building your financial net worth.

As you grow more financially secure, the visions of your childhood come to the forefront. For example, your wife always envisioned she could go on an endless shopping spree and now does, or your husband wants to become a fisherman and goes out and buys all the equipment, including a boat that he uses eight hours per year.

When you attain financial freedom, protect your family nest egg from free-spirited spending. Too many people earn significant amounts of money each year and find nothing left over at the end of the year. As educated as the people in the United States are, it is surprising to me that so many adults are locked into an earn-and-spend way of life. The more they earn, the more they spend. There is no allotment for net worth building. Have the courage to stop the earn-and-spend behavior in your household and break out of the earn-and-spend mode.

Know that with your spending you are striving to be "alive," to locate your individuality, freedom, identity and happiness. Be careful not to mix in compulsive spending. Compulsive, lavish spending only wastes the seed money available for investment. Find happiness with each other, not in madly spending each other's money.

Compulsive spending is a disorder that, if not properly treated, will cause financial frustration and agony to the person and their spouse for a lifetime. Compulsive spending is when spending is taken to an extreme and cannot be controlled, reduced or modified by the person affected. The person afflicted with compulsive spending will deny its existence and insist they could stop spending and begin saving and investing tomorrow if they wanted to. They are driven to spend to counteract stress or depression or other things going on within themselves. If they are having a "blue day," they will go on a shopping spree to find some short-term relief. Much like alcoholics and gamblers, the compulsive spender should be helped with qualified professional counseling to curb and control this difficulty. Compulsive spending is a psychological disorder that needs professional help and counseling.

When your spouse is materialistically oriented, he/she makes demands and makes life difficult until these demands are met. You know the type, the one that needs a Mercedes, jewelry, china, crystal, silver, clothes, over 50 pairs of shoes, boots, skis, fishing and hunting equipment, furniture or the latest electronic equipment.

When someone says, "That's just the way I am, I need expensive things," this is baloney. Such a person can learn to balance and change their belief and demand structure so they are helping to create a solid and healthy financial future within the means of the present household income. Sometimes their attitude comes from an insecure preoccupation with their own individual needs. This type of person is going to keep the family unit from accumulating the necessary capital to start an investment program.

These types of people can be quite helpful net worth builders once they have rechanneled their demand structure. They have the ability to become champion builders once they learn that, if they first make investments and prosper financially, then they will be able get the materialistic things they want. Amassing things slowly over time, these people learn what is of first importance: investments. Investments first. You will want to focus the mind's eye on investments first. Once the investment program is underway and performing well, then these people can purchase their wares, toys and second homes. If these people learn this set of priorities, they will then do one of two things: they will either learn how silly their demands for material things were, or they will continue to buy these material things, but at a more moderate and balanced pace.

While some of these people want material things so badly, when their focus is channeled toward making investments, they can become compulsive, champion builders of net worth. These compulsive spenders for the most part are poor partner choices for those who want to build net worth.

As humans we are equipped with instinct that provides us with automatic direction. We are all striving to stay alive, feel fully alive and express that aliveness. A feeling of aliveness is what we are after with our cars, boats, airplanes, condos, gourmet food and designer clothing.

These compulsive habits need to be balanced through self-discipline or counseling. They are disruptive to the net worth building process. In moderation and balance, they are part of the enjoyment of building net worth.

Some couples spend out of retaliation. If a husband buys a new watch for $800, the wife feels driven to retaliate against the husband and the family checkbook by purchasing a new $1,600 outfit. This kind of competitive spending is not healthy to a marriage relationship and will cause significant damage to the family checkbook. Teamwork, cooperation and harmony while understanding and prioritizing each other's needs is what is required. You should avoid behaviors that bring the family checkbook into a competition and power struggle between the marriage participants. You will want to avoid those behaviors and habits that lead you in the opposite direction to the net worth building process. Adopt the habits and behaviors for net worth building and constantly check that you are steering your family net worth in a positive direction.

Our sense of full aliveness must be tempered. Our free-wheeling energy must be controlled. You must exert some discipline and responsibility in your money management behavior. You need to stop spending and start investing. A similar thrill can come from making a great return on your investments. This sounds regimented, and some have called it boring. When you follow this path and begin explosively building net worth, however, you will be forever grateful that you were mature in your money management behavior and you had some discipline, responsibility and focused energy.

Many adults are putting off marriage until they are age 30 or more. At this age many have seen the marriages of their peer's dissolve. With the thoughts of accumulating wealth combined with the observations of the financially and emotionally painful results of divorce, some adults are deciding not to marry. Instead, they are forming committed long-term relationships.

The committed relationship is the process of recovering feelings of being whole. It is nature's repair process, and this is part of nature's overall design of perpetuation. The relationship provides the opportunity to develop intimacy, love and trust. Single adults who are disappointed in love and past relationships do not want to hear they need a relationship to heal themselves. They want to feel they can be autonomous and restore their wholeness on their own. This is mere delusion. There is much you can accomplish on your own, but you cannot go the whole way to healing childhood wounds without a partner. We need our spouse to fill in the gaps left by our imperfect childhood caretakers.

Consciously we think of finding a mate because we want to have companionship, a special friend, a lover. Really, though, what is happening is the mind is driven by subconscious thoughts to become whole and healthy. Your subconscious carries around a detailed picture of a proper match for you. In this way you are just like a sophisticated guided missile. You have a very clear mental image on board. When someone comes into view through your eyes and there is a match, this is when the fireworks start. When you meet this person, you feel alive and whole.

You hopefully get introduced. You meet, compare notes on likes, dislikes, activities, enjoyments, happiness, wants, needs and desires. As time goes on, you develop friendship and companionship, you become lovers.

You get married because there was a certain attraction flowing both ways. Maybe sparks. Maybe strong friendship. Maybe chemistry. Maybe infatuation, sexual excitement, longing or hormonally induced reactions, a sense of connection, liking, comfort, interest. Early on, you want to be oblivious to each other's faults. Then in about year five of the relationship you want to begin changing and shaping that other person. At this point, what really should be going on is a merging of the physical and mental parts of two people. This combining goes along with forming a unity of purpose.

Once you have merged together completely, you really begin operating as a team. You gain a new understanding of one another. This process has its difficulties, of course, and many times the people do not really merge together. They may live together and learn to put up with one another, but they have not physically and mentally merged to become one within the relationship.

During the course of the marriage, you may feel that one person is striving to control the other. There is within your relationship a struggle for power by both sides. More mature relationship participants are aware of this power struggle and take measures to address it so it does not cause the relationship to suffer. Throughout your relationship your communication skills must be sharpened and opened.

In addressing the communication issues within your relationship, you soon discover the woman speaks in terms of her feelings. The man speaks as if he doesn't have any feelings. These are some well-known man-woman differences that are covered in Chapter 9.

Soon after the commencement of the relationship, you need to learn how the relationship will deal with power, difficulties and struggles. A conflict management department must be present in your relationship. You must agree upon a decent way to fight and work out conflict. The most decent way is through negotiation coupled with open and honest communication. In most cases nothing productive is accomplished with extended shouting matches. With shouting matches out come hurtful words. In the morning you have to apologize for the hurtful words. This apology does not erase the hurt. It is better to get control of your anger, cool off, calm down, then come back and have a decent discussion of the problem area. The book lays out a structured method to conduct that meeting which is far better and less destructive than mean angry hurtful words. Money issues need to be resolved in the relationship through active, open, honest communication. The relationship should not have issues of rivalry toward income contribution. The relationship should have a satisfactory sharing of money management and a reasonable way of settling any disputes over money that might arise. The amount of money you have is less important to the health of your relationship than your method of managing that money. In the relationship, everyone's needs must be met with the resources that are available. Every couple struggles with money issues then eventually there becomes a civil method in which your financial affairs are conducted.

There are successive points in relationships, and people reach them at different rates. Beyond friendship and getting to know someone there should be a shared communication intimacy. Communication intimacy deepens the emotional attachment between two people. It makes you much more willing to reveal your true feelings for the other. As time goes along, both parties should feel safer in the relationship and be willing and available to share their innermost thoughts, dreams, plans and desires. You have to feel safe in the relationship to fully reveal yourself. In order to accomplish this, you have to overcome the fear of intimacy. Keeping secrets works against the attainment of intimacy and inhibits the organic growth of the relationship.

If you share communication intimacy, you should not have any difficulties openly and frankly discussing the details of your family finances.

Many Americans in marriage relationships have some major problems with their communication skills. These people leave too much to fate and chance for the relationship to work out. They have not learned to stop for a moment with their spouse and say, "Honey, we need to practice our communication skills," then commence openly and honestly communicating about the little parts of the relationship that are bugging both of them. Communication is a skill that is made better by continuous practice.

Once you have established a way to practice your communication skills, your family finance topics can enter the conversation without causing much stir.

Face it: you are together because you both want to be together forever. You made certain pledges to one another to be together forever. Do not let little things go uncommunicated until there is some stored-up reason to blow up and leave your marriage. Learn to protect your marriage relationship with good and well-practiced communication skills.

I could tell you hundreds of stories about how married couples deal with money. There are times when a married person does not want to a file joint tax return because they are petrified their spouse will see their earnings. Most married couples do not have a household budget because they could never come to common agreement on what ways and how much to spend in the various categories. Do not risk your relationship by having poor and unused communication skills.

The top 3 factors that will cause divorce

1. Money struggles and battles

2. Sex, sexual intimacy and Infidelity

3. In-law interference

You will want to work on a money flow system that works for your household. Here is what is going on behind the curtain.

7 out of 10 times a spender and a saver are married
2 out of 10 times 2 savers are married
1 out of 10 times 2 spenders are married

Close your eyes and try to figure out the odds of any of these relationships lasting a lifetime.

In broad general terms the spender/saver relationship will work. The two savers will likely divorce due to boredom as they save all the money and don't go out and have fun. The 2 spenders will stay married about 4 years then they are deep in debt and will divorce to be able to start fresh and new!

Communication with your mate becomes easier and easier as you share more and open up more to each other. You will find more joy and more reasons to love your spouse when you frequently communicate openly and honestly. You will relate to one another more abundantly. These are the threads that will take you into a relationship that will last forever.

You are striving to create an intimate bond. Continuing to open up to the other person creates greater depth of attachment, and the bond becomes much stronger. You are ultimately striving to grow a genuine bond of intimate attachment.

Communication intimacy in a married relationship fosters understanding, trust, and emotional connection. It allows partners to openly share thoughts, feelings, and desires, leading to better problem-solving and conflict resolution. Enhanced intimacy strengthens the bond, leading to a happier, more satisfying partnership. Effective communication also promotes empathy and helps couples navigate challenges, ultimately promoting a healthier, long-lasting marriage.

The relationship part of a couple getting together begins when you are no longer dating and have openly announced an extended commitment toward one another. It is at this point the work begins. It requires you to be open and honest with your partner. A relationship requires you to give and to share, to receive and to provide, to nurture and to care. You need to manage your relationship so you can grow together and have a strong, lifetime bond.

In managing your marriage relationship, there are certain killers and keepers that come to surface. Killers are those behaviors that tend to break apart the relationship, lead to conflict, destroy commitment and lead to the dissolution of the marriage. Keepers are those behaviors that lead a person to say they would marry you all over again, those little things that endear your spouse to you for a lifetime. Broadcast keeper behavior and move away from killer behavior. Following are lists of killers and keepers.

KILLERS

Too rigid	Too frigid
Anger	Loner
Incompatibility	Stonewaller
Put-downs	Bad temper
Stubbornness	Infidelity
Workaholic	Fear of success
Self-sabotage	Dishonesty
Inflexible	Secrets
Slob	Poor health
Mental illness	Neglect
Underemployed	Incompetent
Poor social skills	Lack of patience
Destructive criticism	Abusive behavior
Home-building decisions	Needs too much space
Child-rearing differences	Poor sexual partner
Drug or alcohol abuse	Poor discussion leader
Not respecting spouse's privacy	Continuous arguing

Searching through spouse's private property

Intolerant of change in economics

Poor communication skills

Poor conflict management skills

Lack of communication intimacy

Poor or compulsive spending habits

Attempts to control the other person

Blaming the other person

Leaping too quickly into a relationship

Unreasonable expectations

Poor vision of self, the future

No idea how to create wealth independence

Unavailable for open and honest communication

Unable to adjust to adult life
Overly strong ties to parents
Overexposure to relatives

KEEPERS

Seduction

Patience

Kindness

Careful spender

Social grace

Wholesomeness

Generous

Caring

Balanced

Honest

Progressive

Focused

Mature

Responsible

Motivated

Disclosure

Leadership

Morals

Consistent

Commitment

Intelligent

Open to learning new things

Integrity

Punctual

Open communicator

Nurturing

Breadwinner

Positive self-talk

Creative, comfortable nester

Peacemaker

Talented

Sexy

Sensuous

Flexible

Growth oriented

Warmhearted

Complimentary

Congruent

Loyal

Positive mental attitude

Passionate good character

Successful core beliefs

Emotionally mature

The family unit is an organization. The household is an economic unit. Seminar attendees sometimes get up in arms when I tell them the household must be run like a business.

Every corporation has officers and stockholders. There is a president, a vice president and employees. It would be poor management on the part of the officers to allow employees to run the company. It would be difficult for the company to be represented and for final decisions to be made if you could not decide who was going to be the president. Also, the office of president would be harder to have if every day there was a challenger to the job of the president. A person chronically nipping at their heels.

The family unit needs to take on an organizational structure. Parents are the officers, children are the employees. You are all stockholders in your own company/family. Your family can prosper or you can remain lost at sea, it's your choice. Women can be presidents. Men can be presidents. Whoever is president should not have the other spouse constantly saying they are independent people and are going to do as they please every day. In order to have the family unit become successful, you all have to participate and play as a team. This requires team players. This has to be an organized, cohesive unit with every member having a clear description of their duties and responsibilities, operating with a clear unity of purpose in a direction that is going to lead to a better life in the future. This is refrigerator door material!!

The parents are in charge of setting policies and goals and planning the course of the family's financial future. The parents' job is to announce what is expected in a clear statement, then monitor the progress to see that all are on course for your expected target. If you do well, the shareholders will prosper. If you don't do so well, the shareholders all suffer. It's your choice which course to take.

In too many households today the children are running the show. Too many households have a discontented adult emotionally beating and making demands on the other partner rather than stepping out into the world as a unified team to accomplish and get what they want.

The purpose of the marriage relationship is to create a lifelong partnership between two individuals based on love, commitment, and mutual support.

It is a bond where two people come together to share their lives, dreams, hopes for the future and responsibilities. Marriage provides a stable and nurturing environment for raising children, if desired and marriage fosters emotional intimacy and companionship.

In marriage a special connection and bond are created. In marriage, we set out to build a foundation of trust, understanding, mutual respect and shared values. It is a journey of personal growth, where individuals with different priorities and points of view learn to compromise, tolerate, communicate effectively, and navigate life's challenges together to create an environment of harmony within the household.

Romance also plays an important role in marriage. Romance in marriage should be as frequent and more powerful than the romance while dating. In dating the focus is on winning the heart of the other person such that they would consider marriage. Now that marriage has occurred romance needs to continue. Here are some reasons why! Romance and romantic moments play a crucial role in fostering a deep and lasting connection between partners.

Romance ignites passion. It strengthens emotional bonds. Creates cherished memories. Fosters intimacy. Keeps love alive. Sparks excitement. Promotes communication. Adds joy to everyday life. Enhances connection. Shows appreciation. Boosts self-esteem. Creates anticipation. Rekindles desire. Celebrates love. Breaks routine. Builds trust. Nurtures empathy. Encourages vulnerability. Deepens understanding. Promises commitment. Inspires creativity. Surprises and delights. Strengthens resilience. Expresses affection. Sparks laughter. Stirs up adventure. Kindles flirtation. Invites playfulness. Encourages selflessness. Demonstrates thoughtfulness. Embraces spontaneity. Evokes gratitude. Respects individuality. Encourages growth. Revives the spark. Elevates shared experiences. Creates a romantic atmosphere. Builds a sense of security. Affirms love's presence. Promotes physical closeness. Nourishes the soul. Strengthens resilience. Provides comfort. Counteracts stress. Celebrates milestones. Keeps the relationship fresh. Evokes passion. Supports emotional well-being. Sustains long-term love. Makes the journey worthwhile.

The importance of marriage lies in its ability to offer friendship, connection, emotional security, romance, companionship, and a sense of belonging. It contributes to the stability of families and communities, promoting social cohesion and personal happiness.

Ultimately, the purpose of marriage is to create a partnership that enriches the lives of both individuals and researchers say that this strengthens and makes more wholesome the fabric of society.

You need to organize your family unit into a unified team of individuals who understand the main game plan and are all helping to pull in the same direction, each supporting fully the goals and ambitions of the team-family unit and each other.

Every company, every church in America would have a better functioning member of their organization if they did more to encourage and strengthen the fabric of their employees and members marriage.

The purpose of this book is to help you get onto the course and into the spirit of building your financial net worth. From a professional point of view some people need to get help in reprograming their subconscious mind to enable them to participate as a functioning player on the team which has this goal. This way you can work together to carry out the mission of cooperating and participating to accomplish a common goal of building your financial net worth so that all the family members can have a strong financial future. Thus, in this book there is a lot of direction by me to help you see the path and get onto the course and understand it is better when the husband and the wife can work together to help accomplish this goal.

Relationships are complex. Every couple has a different set of needs than another there is no one set relationship. Your relationship needs to be custom made and contoured to your specific needs. Here are some essential elements of a healthy and successful relationship. Let me break down these key factors:

1. **Understanding:** Truly understanding your partner's thoughts, feelings, and perspectives is fundamental. It involves active listening, empathy, and a willingness to see things from their point of view. When both partners make an effort to understand each other, communication improves, and conflicts can be resolved more effectively.

2. **Respect:** Respect is the foundation of any healthy relationship. It means valuing your partner as an individual with their own thoughts, feelings, and boundaries. It involves treating each other with kindness and courtesy, even in moments of disagreement.

3. **Care:** Showing care for your partner's well-being is a way to express your love. This care can manifest in various ways, such as offering emotional support, being there during tough times, and taking steps to make your partner feel special and cherished.

4. **Meeting Needs:** Understanding and meeting each other's needs is crucial. This involves open communication about what each person requires from the relationship and working together to fulfill those needs. It's about creating a balance where both partners feel satisfied.

5. **Mutual Trust:** Trust is the bedrock of a lasting relationship. It's built over time through consistent honesty, reliability, and transparency. When trust is present, both partners can feel secure and confident in the relationship.

6. **Emotional Connection:** A deep emotional connection is what sets a romantic relationship apart from other types of relationships. It's the bond that forms when two people share their innermost thoughts and feelings, creating intimacy and closeness.

By nurturing these factors, couples can indeed foster stable, lasting, and fulfilling relationships. It's also important to note that maintaining a healthy relationship is an ongoing process that requires effort from both partners. Communication, compromise, tolerance and a willingness to grow together are key aspects of long-term relationship success.

MANTRA

I will tell my spouse how special they are to me with a new phrase or kind word every day.

CHAPTER 3

Formula for Financial Success

Goals, vision, drive, intensity and motivation are artistic concepts. They are very real and well known to everyone who has mastered the art of increasing their financial assets into sizeable net worth.

In this chapter we talk seriously about setting goals and creating a clear vision of the future. You will need to know how to utilize these tools if you want to start increasing the size of your financial assets. We will see that growing net worth requires you to have discipline, drive, responsibility and motivation. We all have these. You just need to find and awaken yours within yourself.

To understand success, we must learn what prevents most people from achieving success. The main reason more people are not successful is that they have fundamental fears. You must learn to manage your mind's fear structure in such a way that you will be able to have great financial success. The main fears I see in counseling sessions are fear of success, fear of failure, fear of making a profit and fear of the unknown. Some people manage these fears through a destructive mechanism in the mind called self-sabotage. They can prevent you from becoming a peak performer. People who suffer from this not only sabotage themselves and remain underachievers, but they often also sabotage their mates to prevent them from achieving abundance.

You can begin to see how complex this can get. We discovered in the previous chapter that compulsive spending can be destructive to the net worth building process. Being married to a compulsive spender can lead to financial instability, strained relationships, and emotional stress. The constant overspending can deplete savings, rack up debt, and damage credit scores. Arguments about money can erode trust and intimacy. It may also hinder long-term financial goals, like saving for retirement or buying a home or buying rental property. Seeking professional help and open communication are crucial for addressing these dangers.

Now we see that sabotage can be another component that can be destructive to the net worth building process. If your mate possesses these traits, then you can begin to see how difficult net worth building can be for you. This is why choosing the right mate is very important.

Suffering from fears of abundance will be a roadblock to your financial success and to your success in achieving your status as a peak performer. Your pursuit of excellence and abundance will be much harder than it needs to be.

Many people who work for someone else have formulated ideas that could have made them millions. They never acted on the information they possessed, however. For some reason, they did not go out and start their own business. They did not get themselves into a situation to capitalize on the market shift they saw coming in their industry. Often, the person who has wealth acted on information that gave them keen insight into the marketplace and allowed them to harvest huge profits.(Bill Gates) You, too, can do this. You need the courage to act on the information you possess.

Have the courage to overcome your fears. Find the courage within yourself. Get these obstacles to success behind you. Learn to enjoy prosperity and all the joys and benefits that go along with it.

You must have faith in yourself and focus on how it would feel to have more wealth. In doing this you are using your vision to get an idea of what wealth would look like in your life. You need to focus on where you want to go and what you want to do, not on what you fear. Do not let your fear structure prevent you from getting what is readily available to you. No one is going to go out there and get it for you. You must do it for yourself. You must overcome your fears by knowing that you can accomplish what you set your mind to. For years man has known that if you ask you shall receive, if you seek you will find, if you knock the door will be opened to you. God helps those who help themselves.

All of these are true when you set out to make changes in your habits, ways, beliefs and ideas and you adopt a healthy mental attitude about having and creating wealth and abundance. Having a core belief that you cannot create wealth for any number of reasons is just your way of sabotaging your efforts to create wealth abundantly. Make one list of all the reasons you personally cannot create wealth and a second list of why as a family unit you cannot create wealth. Take the time now to write the reasons down. Make the list as long as you can. While making the list take some time, close your eyes and get down deep within yourself. Make a list of the innermost reasons why you cannot create wealth. Now write these on the sheets of paper you have labeled.

Remember to ask and you will receive. Maximize your gifts and talents, then get focused on what it is you want to do. With determination and staying power, set forth in that direction. With full force, evaluate what results you are getting from your performance and efforts. Then make the course and behavior modifications necessary to accomplish what it is you set out to do.

Your mental computer daily stands ready to serve you. It is capable of great accomplishment if you set it in the right direction and begin to remove the obstacles in its way. You need to move away from the avoidance, denial and sabotage that hold most people back from having the confidence in themselves to build their net worth.

You need to get excited about the idea of net worth building and take action today to move your life in that direction. Get to work. Set out to change your approach, your beliefs and your attitudes. Get the necessary education or information to set your life on the positive path of building an abundant financial future.

Are you making use of your workdays? Are you working to create liquid cash from your earnings to place in investments and real estate? As they grow, these investments and real estate will produce for you a steady stream of cash that will enable you to retire in style.

The more sound the investments you make in stocks, bonds, a family-owned business, mutual funds and rental properties, the more money you will have at your desired retirement age. Memorize this as your recipe for financial security.

There is a catchy concept used by motivational trainers: the concept of "peak performance" individuals.

Peak performance individuals are people who can work with clarity, intensity and focus.

They are able to accomplish a lot with very little. They are resourceful. They use their creativity and ingenuity. They are most likely to learn the process of net worth building.

In setting goals, it is helpful to have role models as inspiration and for information. You will need a mentor. You need to look into the marketplace and find someone out there who you want to be like, someone who has already done it. You need to meet them and see if they would be willing to talk with you from time to time to help you get on course. It is helpful to find someone to emulate. These people can increase your chances for success.

You must possess good judgment and a fair amount of common sense to be successful in business. College degrees and Ph.D. certificates are not needed to be successful in accumulating wealth.

Some of the wealthiest people in the United States are immigrants who could barely speak the English language when they arrived. They bought or started a business, and because they gave it their undivided attention and focused all of their energy on it, the business became a huge success. This tells you that you do not need a fancy education. Though I strongly support education and know for certain that education is the shortcut to success.

These immigrants had motivation. They mainly knew how to do one thing, the business. They knew they had to do it well or the business would fail and they likely would have to return to their country of origin. This kind of attention, focused energy and intensity caused the business to succeed.

If you learn from this example, you, too, can take a business to new heights, enjoying the process and financially prospering along the way.

In business a pound of common sense goes farther than college degrees. You must have the discipline to not be led into temptation by acquiring habits or behavior that is contrary to building net worth.

Although education may be a shortcut to success, balance between education, good judgment and discipline must be present.

Also, you want your children to grow up in the economic system of the free world. You would be doing them a great favor if you would teach them about boundaries and discipline while they are young. Children growing up without a structure of discipline will find it extremely difficult to begin the process of building net worth. Do your children the favor of teaching them how to adopt the behavior necessary to accumulate and preserve wealth. I have not met a child yet who was helped by coming from a household with few rules and little discipline.

Let's get a clear vision of where we are going. We all want to have sufficient financial assets at age 65 to be able to quit work and enjoy the remaining years of our lives without having to work. From my seminars, it is clear that we could get common agreement on this statement. Some people are just able to get there faster than others.

Let's reflect for a few moments. Imagine yourself as you are today. See yourself in your imagination. Imagine you are on a sailboat and sailing in the ocean for a private island where everything is wonderful.

Next imagine you are 100 miles away from that island for every year that you are away from age 65. Thus, if you are 55 (10 years from 65) you are 1,000 miles away (10 years x 100 miles) from landing on the shores of that private island where everything will be wonderful. If you are age 25, you are 4,000 miles away; if you are age 40, you are 2,500 miles away from that private island where everything will be wonderful.

Now if you plan, make strategies and become aware of the environment you will be operating in, you will become successful. You are the skipper of your boat. You are in charge of setting the goals and planning the course for a future landing on the private island. If you plan well, use the tools on board, and make good decisions using your mind and your physical self, you might land on the private island ahead of schedule. You might be able to travel the 4,000 miles in less time than someone who had to travel only 2,000 miles.

Know that the shortest distance between two points is a straight line!

If you do not just sit on your butt and look at the empty pole where the sail is supposed to go, you might get the sails up and use the wind to get on course for the private island.

Being thrown onto a sailboat and told to go in the big ocean would be pretty scary. It would awaken quite a few fears. Some people would learn to work the sails and the tiller. Some people would be content just to slosh around in the ocean, sit back and have a beer, hoping one day the wind would blow them onto the shore of the private island.

Amassing net worth is just like learning to operate a sailboat. You have to learn the system, learn the techniques and gain the necessary information to sail the boat. You need to know when to put up the sails. You need to know when to take the sails down. You need to take hold of the tiller and steer your boat. Grab hold of your life. Doing this is not going to be as difficult as you think. Once you have done it you will look back and say, "Gee, why didn't I do that sooner?"

Life is just like this. If you plan and overcome the fears money brings to everyone, then you will reach your retirement goals much quicker, much happier, and with many more financial resources than you would have had if you had not taken charge and set some goals in life.

While you plan and adopt goals to set you on a straight line for your private island, that grand retirement place where life is wonderful and financially worry-free, the winds of life can and will blow. Events, casualties, family crises, tragedies, catastrophes and emergencies are going to occur and cause financial setbacks as you head for your private island. These events will blow you off course.

In life you must learn to rebound, recover and rise to the occasion.

You need to be equipped with the necessary information and navigational aids and skills to adjust, rebound, recover and get back on course. These tools are many, and most of them are sitting down at your local library. You need to get down there and pry the information out of reference books. Failure to read is the sure way to be left behind in this age of high technology and information. Failing to read books about investments, real estate and financial news is like sitting at sea and failing or refusing to look at the map because you already know where you are going. This stubbornness and refusal to look at the details on the chart are what separate the high achievers from the low achievers in life.

Your mind is the tool that will help you amass financial assets. Your mind is your most valuable asset. It can help you reach your financial goals quickly and easily. Take care of it. Feed it, exercise the body that is the support system for the brain, and exercise the brain by reading. This will lead to new ideas and new techniques. Feed your subconscious by reading about people's financial success. Read about investments and building winning strategies. Feed your subconscious with these positive inputs.

The more common sources of information are parents, teachers, peers, television, radio, newspapers, magazines, videos, movies, tapes and advertisers. Go to your magazine rack in your home and look at the inputs you have been feeding your brain. If the rack is empty, this tells you something right away. If the rack is full of recipe books, you might

FORMULA FOR FINANCIAL SUCCESS / 33

be having great meals on board your boat in life, but this is not going to get you where you want to be financially.

You may now want to monitor and filter these inputs so you can update the programming of your mind to things that are positive and directed, inputs that are goal oriented and focused on where you want to be in your vision of an ideal relationship and an ideal life in your retirement years.

Something that might help you is to make a vision board. Use an ordinary cork bulletin board. Cut out magazine pictures that represent your future. Pin up photographs of the area or house you would like to live in, the vehicles or toys you would like to own, the clothes you want to wear. When your vision board is completed to your liking, put it up where you can see it every day. Your mind will see the pictures daily and begin leading you in that direction.

> Do not try to mimic or model your parents' day-to-day life. They may not have provided those positive inputs needed to be successful.
>
> Do not be caught in a keelless boat.
>
> Do not be caught in life without written goals for focusing your energies.
>
> Do not be caught with a financially incompatible partner.
>
> Do not allow destructive habits to continue in your household.
>
> Do not allow your children to enter the world ill-equipped to manage and grow financial assets.
>
> Do not become a ship lost at sea, at any age.

You need to tune up your self-confidence and sense of well-being. If you have a good image of yourself and high self-esteem while being at peace with yourself, then you can be at peace with others. This is necessary to channel the focused energy you need to get on the straight line to success. Being at peace will enable you to sow the seeds of success. You do not have to allow the programming of your past to control your present and future life.

You must have goals. When you set goals, you then have a target, a spot you can focus on. When you focus on that spot, you can channel all of your energies in that direction. Once on course, you can increase the intensity of your energies to meet your target ahead of schedule.

Your mind is always looking for something to do. Some people have anesthetized their minds; they have put their minds to sleep. They mechanically get up and go about their day, then are usually glued to the television at night, then get up and repeat this cycle each day for many years. They do this until they realize it is high time, they wake up their mind. Like an unexercised muscle, the mind begins to come back. These people begin to read. They begin to broaden their horizons. They get in contact with new ideas. Then all of a sudden one day it all comes together and they get the great idea that it is time to take charge of their financial future.

Once this occurs, they are ready to set goals, to make plans, to chart the course and then travel in the direction of financial success. Once in motion, it is much like planning for a road trip to a land they have not been to before. The sense of adventure and discovery comes to life. The plans begin to materialize. Daily goals of how far they are going to travel get put in writing. The trip soon is going to become a reality. The information is gathered and the plan is ready; it is time to spring into action.

This is what it is like to come alive again and believe in your own financial future. You are the designers of your life together. Get off the couch and start living.

In our office, it is quite fun to finish a series of counseling sessions with older people and see their joy as they discover that financial abundance can be theirs, too. They begin to make plans, and those plans lead to other ideas. Soon they are excited and enthusiastically in pursuit of their newly adopted goals.

Setting goals is the first step you take in making your financial dreams become a reality. Goal-setting is the way you get your mind to focus on and move you in the direction you have planned. Setting goals will allow you to experience personal growth. By doing this, you turn the invisible into the visible. Then your mind can go to work in taking you where you want to be. You need to feed your mind with the fuel of daily positive inputs that are going to keep you on course and get you to where you want to be.

In setting goals, you want to take these steps:

1. Make an honest, factual assessment of where you are today by making a list in dollars and cents.

2. Create a vision of your future by visualizing where you want to be, what you want to have and when you will get there. Make a specific list of the items you envision in your future. List your dreams, wants, needs and desires. Let this be a fun time listing all the things you ever wanted.

3. Set specific written goals with the day, date and time you plan to get there.

4. Adopt and use the necessary tools that will get you to where you want to be. Adopt a specific financial management system that includes a monthly written report. Obtain additional information and education as needed to supplement your plan.

5. Commit to being available to make the changes in your life to get to where you want to be. Making changes are the growth steps you take in making your life better and more complete. Drop any habits that detract from your ability to build your net worth. Be open to developing attitudes and strategies that will bring you abundance.

6. Write down your one-year plan, your five-year plan and your ten-year plan. Share these written plans with your partner and ask for their support in reaching your goals.

Setting goals and putting your goals in writing are helpful because you both can see and focus on the same goals. If you do not put your goals in writing, you will continue pursuing your goals and your spouse will be doing the same. There likely will be a lot of tugging and pulling going on rather than the harmony that can accompany two people truly in love, working happily toward the same set of goals.

Some people have set goals in the past and failed to reach them. To avoid further disappointment, they refuse to set new goals. This is foolish behavior. You need to awaken your drive to achieve your goals. With a road map you might get there. If you do not reach the place you want to be, you must try and try again.

If you meet an obstacle in life, do not try to get over that obstacle by repeating an approach that does not work. Life is like a maze sometimes. Do not attempt to keep jumping into the air over and over again to get over the wall in the same place. Drop back and form a new plan. Try to run and jump over the wall. Try to hop, skip and then jump over the wall. Try to climb the wall with a rope. Try to scale that wall with your creativity and ingenuity. Try and try until you succeed.

All of the great Americans who have prospered in business in a big way can tell you stories of how they tried and tried before finally succeeding. I can assure you that none of them went out there with their first attempt and built up a company, became financially successful and then retired happily ever after. This only happens in nursery rhymes and storybooks. In reality, you must try and try again to scale that wall. In doing so you might jump high enough to expand your vision and then be able to see the gate on your right-hand side; then instead of jumping and jumping to get over the wall you simply move to your right, open the gate and move to the other side of the wall that was your obstacle. Obtaining financial success follows this pattern. You must make the commitment to try and try again, because if you do, financial abundance will strike your household and your wildest dreams will come true.

Unless you have definite, precise, clearly set goals, you are not going to realize the maximum potential available in your future. You will be like a sailboat without a keel. You will be washed ashore onto the beaches of despair, depression and defeat. You will be washed up on the beach and will have to fight the waves to get back out to sea in pursuit of the private island again. Some people will never make it past the breakers. Some will not be able to muster the effort, energy and information to get past the waves. Don't get caught in this effortless mode with your life plans. Some people love to live day-to-day without thought or direction. Some operate as if they have had a frontal lobotomy (a portion of the brain removed). Stand up and take charge of your life. Make plans to gain a direction for your financial future that you control.

A written plan is the best plan. How many of you would jump in the car and head a thousand miles to a distant city without taking a map with you? Would you do this? You would not do this in your car, you would not do this with your boat, but people every day are willing to travel through life without a map, without a plan. Why is this?

Remember, most people do not plan to fail, they fail to plan.

You must routinely put your goals in writing. Goal-setting requires you to reflect on the future. You must take a position. You must say, "I want to be somebody important, I want to do something with my life. I want to become accomplished, and I want to add something to this world in which I live."

You must have a positive image of yourself. You must want to get somewhere with your life. You must understand the business world enough to conduct your affairs in a prosperous way.

Deciding not to call the pizza delivery man more than twice per week for a year is not the kind of goal-setting that will help you prosper financially. Set goals that will bring and encourage financial prosperity. You must have a list of goals. If you find it difficult to establish your goals, spend an hour annually with a professional who can help you.

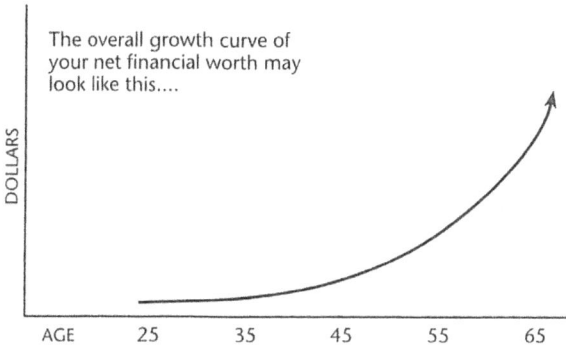

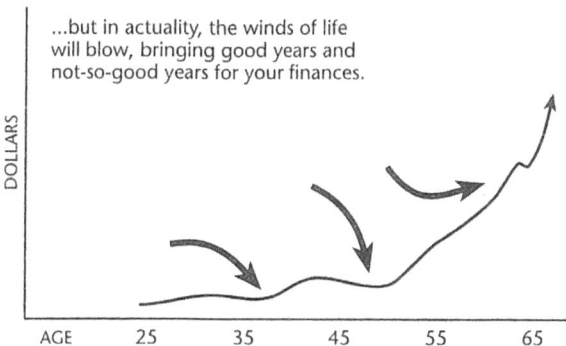

The overall growth curve of your net financial worth may look like this....

DOLLARS

AGE   25   35   45   55   65

...but in actuality, the winds of life will blow, bringing good years and not-so-good years for your finances.

DOLLARS

AGE   25   35   45   55   65

Take some time right now! Get a blank sheet of paper and write down your financial goals for this current year. Take another sheet of paper and write down your financial goals for the next five years, and one more sheet of paper for your financial goals over the next ten years. Do this now. Do not let procrastination play a part in your life any longer. When you are finished, compare lists with your mate. Try to consolidate and prioritize your goals so you both have one unified set of common goals.

Remember,goals provide a clear destination for financial success, serving as a roadmap to follow. Vision is the long-term perspective that guides goal-setting, inspiring individuals to strive for more. Drive fuels the relentless pursuit of those goals, pushing through obstacles and setbacks. Intensity involves focused effort, channeling energy into productive actions. Motivation is the inner fire that sustains these efforts, rooted in personal desires and ambitions. Together, these elements create a powerful formula for financial success, driving individuals to set ambitious goals, maintain a clear vision, stay committed, work intensely, and draw strength from their inner motivation to achieve their financial aspirations.

Wealth building is about winning in life. In order to do it you need to outfox the competition. You need to do something unique. You need to take something that works and add your ten percent. Many Americans are too timid to be winners. If you want to be a winner in life, the inputs you provide your subconscious mind are very important. Be sure you have a program for putting winning information into your subconscious mind.

It would be helpful to you and your spouse to take a few moments at this time to write down on another sheet of paper what "winning" means to you. Do this quietly and separately. Compare your response to that of your spouse. Note that you have different responses. Discuss your response with your spouse, then try to make one list that provides the definition of "winning" for your household. Write down you mutual relationship goals.

MANTRA

I will submit my written goals to my mate twice a year and follow up by consolidating those goals into one unified list.

CHAPTER 4

Roadblocks to Successful Money Management

You must learn to overcome the obstacles. The experiences of childhood have brought you to where you find yourself today. Unless you have noticed them, made changes and healed, you are not likely to have a well-balanced adult life that includes financial prosperity and net worth building.

You need to take notice in order to overcome these subconscious implants. You must be consciously aware of what you want in life. Then you are on your way to controlling your own destiny.

You must take steps to control your own destiny. Do not risk your life to fate or chance or merely let yourself be propelled by the winds of life. Dig in and make a commitment in life. Take charge of your life, stand up on your own two feet and stand for something. Make a commitment to financial prosperity. You are an adult with a mind capable of great accomplishment. Do not be convinced you cannot achieve financial success because your parents were unable to do so. Many Americans suffer from this syndrome. Each one of us has the power and capability to be quite successful in life. Fortunately, we do not all possess the same qualities, gifts, talents and aptitudes. We are all different. You need to awaken to and capitalize on the gifts you were given. Do not anesthetize them like many others have. Take charge of your life. Set attainable goals. Conserve and build wealth from the bottom up and savor your successes when you retire before you reach age 65.

Close your eyes and see what you would look like if you had substantial wealth. Then step out and reach that point you can visualize. Design a plan that works for you and your household. Get the quality of life your imagination directs you toward. Do not envy the neighbors. Get out there and do it. Take steps to build net worth and achieve your financial freedom. With determination, commitment, focus and a strong sense of where you are going—based on well-laid-out plans, goals, opportunity and achievement—you can decide to have financial freedom well beyond your wildest imagination.

Visualization is a method of opening your mind and removing your self-imposed limitations and restrictions in order to get a picture of a life of abundance and prosperity. As you open your mind, you create a positive mental image of what the results are going to be. Visualization is a very powerful tool.

If you do not get there, it is only because you hold yourself back from this accomplishment. You have the ability, time and opportunity. You need to focus or channel your energies in the right direction to get what you really want from life. Many people do not get to where they want to be financially and sit back with envy of those who did. Don't do this. You have the time. From age 25 to 65 you have 40 years for accomplishment. You need to move your life in the right direction to get there.

Go to a resort area and look at the expensive homes. They are all owned by someone. You, too, can get what you want from this world financially. You need to jump out of the back seat into the front seat. Gain the necessary information to drive the car, control the gas and work the gears. Once empowered with information, you will be unstoppable in your quest for financial reward. You are in charge. You need to control your own destiny.

It has been said many times that our population is made up of people who:

1. Make it happen
2. Watch it happen
3. Wonder what happened

Take charge now and pick the one category that has the greatest chance of moving you in the direction of attaining great financial success.

Wealth builders know that any product or service in the marketplace can be improved. To make a million dollars on any product or service, all you have to do is improve upon that product or service by 10%.

You do not need to invent something from scratch. Build upon what is already there. If you can invent something new, you have the chance of even greater fortunes. Channel your time and energy into something that is going to improve upon what is already here.

Some successful companies create goods and services that increase the quality of life for all the customers they serve. If you help others get what they want, you will end up getting what you want. Get focused, set your goals, gain the necessary information, devise a plan of implementation and move forward into the winner's circle. You will need to be unobstructed, to overcome any paralysis generated by your own on-board computer. You must train the subconscious to accept abundance and success and to seek this out in life. Call upon your determination to guide you on the path to financial freedom.

Take the time to turn your dreams into reality. Determination is the commitment to follow the plans you have focused on. Determination is the power that takes you from where you are and puts you ahead where you want to be. You need to awaken and get in touch with your determination. Determination is the overwhelming power that drives you in the direction of your commitment. By being a good competitor, you allow your determination to work for you. With your determination firmly set, you can accomplish anything. You need to have the courage to stand up and take charge of your life and to head in the direction of financial prosperity.

Along with determination, energy and intensity are needed in your vision for financial success.

Men who have physical impotency get medical treatment. Some people set goals that are impotent with regard to building their net worth. Then they give up. You need to set realistic goals that are going to lead you in the direction you want to go with your financial life. If these goals do not get you to where you want to be, you need to conduct a reassessment. Then try again, constantly being flexible enough to make changes until you get what you want.

Financial goals will be quite different for everyone. You need to set goals that are achievable by you. Your goal could be to save $1,000 per year toward your child's college education. Your goal could be to purchase another rental property every five years. Your goal could be to earn $100,000 per year. The fun in life is designing your own goals. Set goals you can achieve. Set goals that put you ahead in life. You must set daily goals that link to weekly goals. Then set weekly goals that link to monthly goals. Set monthly goals that link to annual goals. Then set annual goals that work into your five-year plan. This is how you approach your goals. Your goals must be written, and you must give your written goals to your spouse or someone close to you who can help support you in reaching your goals. Set goals that are clear and specific.

With your goals mapped out in writing, you will move with mental clarity in the direction of success. It is amazing how fast we can move toward success with a set of written goals. These goals become more powerful and are more easily attained when we have provided a copy of our written goals to our spouse and called upon our spouse to support us in our efforts to reach our goals.

If you have made goals and you have not attained them, you should consider changing your approach to reaching those goals. Sometimes we approach things with a personality that could stop a clock. Know that it is not the system that is wrong; usually it is your personal approach to the system that is wrong.

> **You need to get in touch with your mental, emotional, physical, spiritual and financial self. When you open the doors to these powerful channels and let health flow in, you are properly aligned to achieve success.**

If you give it a try and you do not immediately meet with success, you need to have the fortitude and determination to stick with it. A great example of this is the baseball player Hank Aaron. He has international fame as a successful person. He unquestionably was a very successful baseball player. He added his 10% and more to the game of baseball. He always played with focused energy at 110% effort when he took the field. Many people know him for the 755 home runs he hit. Not many people know that in order to hit all of those home runs Hank Aaron had to strike out over a thousand times. If you strike out in your quest, gather yourself and come back to the playing field on another day to give it another try. Be flexible in your approach. Modify your approach if you are not meeting with the success you designed.

**If you want to be successful, you will have to let go
of the negative programming of your childhood.**

Your belief structure today is the net result of what you were taught by your parents. Your parents did the initial programming of your mental computer. You may need to update or change the programming in your computer to get onto the road of financial success. Your parents guided you through your childhood years. You need to evaluate for yourself what beliefs you want to carry into your future. The sooner you can let go of what you carry around unnecessarily from the past, the faster you can run into your future. It can save you many hours of counseling if you can let go of the baggage from your past. Set your goals and live today for the future. Combine your accumulated skills and abilities with the tuned horsepower of your on-board computer. Be a pioneer and a leader, paving the way for a better tomorrow for you and your children.

You have to take responsibility for your own actions. Your place in life is a result of the encounters you have had and the decisions you have already made. If you want your course to change, you have to take responsibility for your life today. You cannot blame anyone for your position in life. It is unfortunate that with abuses, tragedies and misfortunes, there becomes damage to our minds, bodies and emotions. You must take responsibility for your place in life today. Blaming someone else shows that you do not have a healthy, adult sense of responsibility. Forget your past. Who are you today? Unload your excess baggage and begin feeling alive today. Pull from your competitive spirit to activate your energies and enthusiasm for life. Power up your determination by making a commitment to accomplish what you focus on.

Some people cannot stand up and accept the results of their decisions. They cannot accept where they are in life. They must blame everyone else for their lack of financial prosperity.

Achieving financial prosperity is for everyone. It is available to everyone. Net worth building can be fun. It does not matter if you are starting from the ghetto, with or without a college education, or from a family of low economic means, middle income or wealth. This is America. Anyone can adopt a product or service to perform and do it better than someone else. You have to tap into the gifts you have been provided and utilize them to take full advantage of the income that is available to you. You need to work at it by working smart, not by working hard.

As I travel around the country, it is always interesting to hear the reasons why people believe they cannot build their financial net worth. After these people hear the reasons coming from their own mouths, they seem to instantly get the idea that they, too, can build net worth. They hear their own excuses and know they cannot continue on the path they are on. They seem to self-adjust with the assistance of the information that my Net Worth Building Seminar provides them. This seminar tells how to get on course to financial prosperity.

It is too bad that through the various types of advertising media we receive the daily association of gaining freedom by purchasing consumer goods. Commercials are all designed to get you to purchase consumer goods. Too bad they do not teach you to save your money first, build financial freedom and then pursue purchasing consumer goods. If the government imposed a one-year moratorium on consumer goods commercials and only investment companies ran advertisements— sexy, zesty, fun, action advertisements on what were good products in which to invest—the majority of the American people would be rushing out to purchase advertised investments. Please notice how you respond to inputs you receive throughout the day. If you want to train yourself to invest, you must seek out positive inputs to help you become a good investor.

Please take the time now to make another list of the things that prevent you from building your financial net worth. Make the list as long as you can. Give some deep, soul-searching thought to this exercise. Stop now and write down your list.

In order to adopt a program of work that is going to take you in the direction of building net worth, you have to be open-minded and willing to commit to making changes in the method you presently use to manage your money. If you are not building your net worth, your money management techniques must not be working. Humans can do anything they put their minds to. To move in that direction, you must be open and willing to make changes.

Once you have made your list and are open and willing to make changes, prepare another list of how you see yourself moving in the direction of becoming a champion net worth builder. Take some time and make this written list now.

If you really have courage, you can share your lists with your spouse. This is an exercise to help you, but it is not necessary to discuss your list with your spouse at this time.

If you want to change financially, you must know that something about the way you presently manage your money must change. You must be the one who makes the shift necessary for change to occur. You must know you have the power within you to make that change now, because you have to be the source of your change.

It seems that if year after year you end up with the same result, your salary in and your salary out with no investment program started, you might be willing to make changes and shift to a direction that would allow you to build net worth. If you continue in this same mode, you will earn and spend your whole career away. If this is your pattern, if this is you, then this message should send a strong signal to you about breaking your habits and patterns and then taking a different approach to your finances. Then you could be building something rather than constantly depleting your resources.

You need to search out a pattern that leads to financial health and prosperity, then position yourself to enjoy the result.

The end of each chapter has a mantra. You should skip to the end of each chapter and write down each mantra on something you take with you each day. You should allow these mantras to enter your daily life. You should repeat aloud each mantra three times each morning and three times each evening. You can do this in the car with the windows rolled up each day on your way to work. It is a proven drive-time technique. Some people have invented their own songs about each mantra, and rather than speak the mantras, they sing them in the car each day. This is positive input to give yourself on a daily basis. It is amazing how well it helps lead you in the direction of building financial net worth. You want to commit to becoming a champion net worth builder.

Much of our inability to become financially free stems from our childhood roots. The core of your present-day beliefs originated there. I put forth the idea of inspecting your childhood if you are having trouble developing net worth building plans. I am not condoning hours of blaming your parents. Instead, understand that you cannot un-spill the milk. Forgive your parents and move on to building success in your life.

Motivational training can be very helpful in getting you on the road of net worth building. There are many self-help selections available that supplement this book. You should have a routine of listening and reading self-help publications frequently. This feeds the mind with positive inputs that help you attain a greater degree of success in your endeavors.

We use our brains to plan, organize, invent, create, compute, design, analyze, form strategies and make decisions. The brain basically has two departments: the conscious mind and the subconscious mind. It is the subconscious mind that has a powerful effect on our ability to create and amass financial order, financial security and increased net worth.

To fully grasp who we are, where we are going and what motivates us, we have to go beneath the surface and look at the subconscious.

The subconscious mind is a very powerful tool that is always working. If we can feed our subconscious mind positive thoughts about health and happiness in our relationship, about prosperity and abundance in family finances, then we have the potential to be powerful people capable of huge success and accomplishment within our lifetime.

Thus, you must feed your subconscious mind often with positive, helpful inputs. You learn from repetition.

Find some self-help tapes. Listen to different authors, then buy more of the author whose style is most compatible with yours. Find an author's style you enjoy and follow their tapes and books. Relisten and reread them often. This means more than once! You and your subconscious will find them inspirational and motivational.

One relaxation tape is a must. Allow yourself to go into a deep trance as you experience relaxation. This awakens many creative capabilities.

One of the biggest roadblocks to financial success is fear. It has a range of levels, from mild worry to fright and terror. We must learn to manage our fear structure. There are many types of fear that people put forth as reasons why they cannot move in the direction of greater financial prosperity. Fear is a major obstacle for some people. Fear is something that must be confronted. You cannot have fear and succeed to the upper echelon of wealth accumulation.

Each time you experience fear, a few days later reflect upon whether the feeling of fear was necessary. Chart those incidences in which you have feelings of fear. Look at your list 30 days later. Try to plan to deal with the situation without experiencing fear.

Some motivational instructors have defined fear as:

F	False
E	"Empressions"
A	Appearing
R	Real

Give this some thought and see if it helps you in overcoming your fears. Now give it some deeper thought. Now see if it helps you in overcoming your fears in life.

You must overcome the fear of setting goals or the fear of forging ahead. Do not worry that you will make some wrong or bad choices or decisions. These will become learning experiences. You grow stronger and stronger after each learning experience.

In accumulating wealth, you learn by doing things. Lack of action or sitting back because you have the fear of failure; fear of your abilities, talents and special gifts; fear of making a profit; fear of taking action; or some other fear structure and paralysis will not help you produce increased net worth. Overcoming fear is a very important step in accumulating and protecting your financial assets.

Besides fear, there are additional roadblocks to your financial success. These are lack of education, lack of business experience and business naivety. Many people suddenly come into money one way or another: the lottery, a large court settlement, an inheritance, a large bonus, collection on an insurance policy or whatever. These people are classified as windfall recipients. Although there are no national statistics available, our office surveys show that, within five years, eight out of ten of these people will lose all the money they received. It amazes me. Each year so many people come into money that could be the foundation and cornerstone of their investment program. Rather than seek out good investments that are balanced and suited to them, these people waste the money at every turn. First, they go on a spending rampage. Then they turn to investments far too risky for their education and background, hoping they will triple their money in a short period. Sometimes they go into real estate far over their head. Then some try to buy a business and fail to gain the necessary information to run the business. Some set out in business to be more brave and less conservative than their parents, only to lose all of their money.

The important thing to know is that investing and business are difficult if you have not had the proper exposure. If you inherit or come into new money, plan to conservatively invest the new money so it will grow and grow. If you plant that seed properly, you will have a huge retirement nest egg from those funds, a nest egg that is big and beyond your wildest imagination. Hang onto that money; do not sell your house. Stay where you are. Grow into another house with the resources from your career earnings. Invest the new money conservatively and wisely so it will pay off big time when you are older.

Parents should understand that if children (including adult children) come into money they have not earned, eight out of ten times they will lose that money. Parents are wise to put that money into a trust, out of the reach of the children's creditors and out of the reach of divorce courts. Require the trustee to invest the monies wisely and disburse only the earnings until the children reach a certain age, an age at which they would be less likely to waste it. Then have the trust begin to release the principal you have left for them, stretching out the principal amounts released over a long period of time. Design the trust to provide retirement funds and income for your child so they may retire in style.

You must not let your fear outpace your desire for success. You are the designer. If I were you, I would make the decision to outbalance fear with a desire for success, using the recipe of one part fear, a hundred parts desire, focus, commitment and determination.

Fear can serve as a motivator, pushing you to make prudent financial decisions, like saving for emergencies or investing wisely to avoid potential setbacks. Desire fuels ambition, inspiring you to set and achieve financial goals, whether it's buying a home or starting a business. Focus helps you stay on track, enabling you to allocate resources efficiently and avoid distractions that may hinder financial growth. Commitment ensures you stick to your financial plans over the long term, resisting the temptation to splurge or deviate from your objectives. Determination empowers you to overcome obstacles and setbacks, fostering resilience in the face of financial challenges. Combined, these qualities can help you steadily build your financial net worth, securing a more stable and prosperous financial future.

MANTRA

I will work at overcoming my fears every day.

CHAPTER 5

Financial Freedom

Where are we going? This is a question many married couples should ask themselves, and often. How and when do you want to get there? This is the second question you should ask yourselves.

Many families have found their financial freedom through their family-owned business. Family-owned businesses can be started from scratch or by purchasing a business someone else started.

Family-owned businesses are not for everyone. You must be prepared to work long hours to get the business off the ground. Once started, you can then reap the rewards by not having to work so long or so hard in later years. Once self-employed, I do not know many people who would consider becoming an employee of a company again.

The business usually takes on a resale value. You can sell the business one day to someone else, usually at a substantial profit. The increase in value of the business adds to your annual net worth.

If you have interest in being an entrepreneur you should take a look at a book that is a cousin to this book, *Entrepreneurship-Believe & Achieve*, this book will supply you with powerful information and a briefing of what you will encounter if you want to become self-employed.

If you are planning to open a business, it might be a little easier to purchase the business from someone who gave it a try. Make sure the business has the potential to earn the amount of profit you want. It can be helpful to seek the services of a business broker to help you locate the type of business and location you want. There are business brokers available for mom-and-pop businesses. There are business brokers who can help you acquire a complete division of a company that plans to spin off a segment of its business. Make inquiries with the business professionals that serve your needs.

Some people have become quite proficient at buying businesses and sprucing them up. They apply their talent to make the company run better. Once running better, the business is sold at a very substantial profit. Some people do this on a regular basis, selling one business and buying a new business every three years. You have to do this in accordance with what is comfortable to you.

Some people are great at getting businesses off the ground, but day-to-day management is not for them. Some people like to purchase a going business so all they have to do is the day-to-day management, which is what they like to do and what they do best. You have to know your own strengths and weaknesses, what captures your interest, what is boring to you. We are all unique people who like and enjoy different things.

Some businesses are not resalable, for instance, certain professional practices or businesses that require the specific talent of a specific person. A customer base is usually what is sold, customers accustomed to purchasing your goods or services. It is the steady stream of orders and customers and movement of your goods and services that make the business resalable. Investigate and research before you start your business. Be sure your business is resalable if you want to pursue this avenue.

For years, to my amazement, courts have been awarding large amounts of money to divorcing spouses for practices that are not resalable. This incongruity is incomprehensible. If the courts are dividing property, it should be a division of property that has an identifiable fair market value. A division of property should not be awarded based on some fiction the judge read in a book. There have been awards for businesses such as a surgeon's practice, when there has never been a sale of a professional practice of this kind.

You should analyze the business before you enter into it.

Most manufacturing and food-processing businesses put 45% effort into production, 45% effort into sales and 10% effort into administrative chores.

Carefully analyze this formula. It is very rare to see a family-owned business with the correct balance of talent and effort in both manufacturing and marketing. Usually a family-owned company is strong in manufacturing the product or in marketing the product. If your strength is manufacturing, then you have to cope with the marketing chores, honing them so the company grows in a direction that enhances marketing. If your strength is marketing, then you have to cope with the manufacturing chores, honing those so the company grows in a direction that makes it better at manufacturing. You will need to strive to have a company that is whole and complete. You will want to have a company that is great at manufacturing and great at marketing, and you must be eager and willing to work in that direction with all members of the business. Oddly enough, as a business consultant I can tell you not many family-owned businesses are whole and complete in this way. If someone were sharp, all they would have to do is acquire out-of-balance businesses and make them whole and complete. If you presently own a business, seek the proper professional consultants who can verify that your business is now operating as a whole and complete business enterprise.

Seize upon all available opportunities. Look for a company that is strong on production, weak on marketing. Buy it and add your marketing skills. Look for companies that are strong on marketing and weak on production, then add your production skills.

Large, publicly owned companies have been known to buy "George's Potato Chip Company," for example, for millions of dollars. Numerous family-owned business are purchased by large companies for millions of dollars. Large companies do not want to take the initial risk to see if a product will really work in the marketplace. They want to sit back and watch your product move in the marketplace. Then they become interested. If you are a good business deal maker, you, too, can sell your company for millions of dollars.

Be aware that many greenhorns to business have tried to start one of these companies by obtaining investor capital raised through family or by way of limited partnerships. Once the company was really working, the young greenhorns were thrown out of the business on a technicality and the family, friends or investors took over just long enough to sell the company at a substantial profit.

Do not enter into any business arrangement without being properly represented by your own lawyer and certified public accountant. Require that both of these professionals read each and every agreement before you sign it.

When possible, have your own lawyer draft all documents.

CAPITAL AND MANAGEMENT OF THE BUSINESS

Most family-owned businesses fail within the first five years. These failures can be traced back to two primary causes:

1. Lack of capital

2. Bad management decisions

Now that you know this, do not become the next business casualty.

In terms of capital, you must have enough money to start and sustain the business. This means you have to do all of the necessary building improvements and equipment purchases to first open the doors for business. Before you start your business, you must also have enough money on hand to pay for monthly costs and overhead for four months.

The primary reason you see businesses struggle to start, open for two months and then close is that they have insufficient start-up capital. Not only do you need to secure a location to conduct the business, you need to buy the tools and equipment necessary to operate the business and a sufficiency of working capital to operate the business through its infancy.

The work of the entrepreneur is to survive. Many people start businesses in their homes or garages and then move the business into larger quarters as it begins to grow. The point is, you need to have a sufficiency of working capital at the time you start the business to help the business through its infancy.

After you have nurtured the business through its early stages, you must then have at all times a contingency reserve of cash available to you for the rest of your business life. This money comes from earning a profit from the business and putting a portion of the profit into your savings account. Then if a business bump or unforeseen cost of business occurs, you will not be forced out of business. Too many businesses operate without a structured amount of money as a cash reserve. With a cash reserve, your business will operate much smoother and with less stress and frustration.

It is very unlikely that your business will earn a profit within the first six months of operation. Thus, you must have sufficient cash reserves to cover each one of the areas of start-up costs. Starting with less is very foolhardy. This is one reason many businesses start in someone's garage. Hewlett-Packard Company, makers of fine computer and computer-related equipment and instruments, started off in a garage. Its products are now known worldwide.

In terms of management, you must know enough about what you are doing to make decisions that help your business grow in a positive direction. If you make too many bad decisions, you are out of business.

This doesn't mean you have to graduate from a famous business school. It means you need to learn about the business and the industry in which it operates. Good management skills require you to possess a great deal of regular common sense. You need to be ready to plan, organize, operate, staff, direct and control the business. Equipped with good management skills and common sense, you will be ready to get your business going. Management duties require you to plan, organize, staff, evaluate and orchestrate the operational details of your business.

Any basic business course will teach you that being a great car mechanic does not necessarily mean you will be a great businessperson, being a great chef will not necessarily make you a great restaurant owner. If you are a car mechanic and decide to go into business for yourself, you will soon learn you cannot work on all the cars, service the customers' needs and take care of all the administrative tasks of the business. You will have to staff the business with workers who can be trained to do various jobs. You will have to be a great car mechanic and a good business manager. You will have to properly plan for the needs of the business and for the needs of your customers. You will have to learn how to get new jobs and complete the existing jobs in a timely manner. In doing this, you may soon find that you have very little time to work on cars yourself. You will have to learn to work the controls of the business so you will earn a profit.

There are some good idea people out there and some good detail people out there. In order to manage a business, you need to be both. You have to be a big idea type who can visualize the business on a grand scale. You have to be a detail person who can attend daily to the chores and needs of the business. Balance is a requirement. Successful businesses are not run by one or the other of these people. Successful businesses are run by people who have someone in charge of the big picture and someone in charge of the small details.

If you are thinking of starting a business, know you will have to be surrounded by top-quality professionals. The ongoing professionals you will need are a banker, a lawyer, a CPA and an insurance person.

Banker: You should take great pains to be introduced to and acquainted with your banker. You should find the main branch of a commercial bank in your town and then locate the highest bank official that will talk with you. Be sure you are banking at the main branch of the bank. Ask them if they are available to be your banker. If you are self-employed, you need to make time, on a weekly basis, to go to your bank. As often as possible, stop by the manager's desk to say hello and give an update on what's happening with your company.

Consider taking your banker out to lunch as your guest. This will allow you to dialogue and network with your banker. You will get to know each other much better, and this has many benefits. Most bankers are encouraged by the bank to take customers to lunch, but they rarely do. The customer should be looking for ways to get to know their banker. When you ask, "Do you have time for lunch?," most often the banker will enthusiastically answer "Yes." You must be the catalyst in building a strong banking relationship. Banking is conducted in the relationship form of business.

> **Take great pains to become acquainted with your banker. You must develop a great banking relationship if you want to be successful in business.**

There is a good reason for becoming friendly with your banker. One day after you have started your business, you will need a loan, usually an equipment loan and an open line of credit. If the banker knows you are a good-quality person, the loan process will go much, much smoother.

If you think a banker will make you a loan to start your business, forget it. They won't. They do not provide start-up capital, unless you have collateral to offer in order to secure the loan.

Lawyer: Yep, you need one. The cost of a lawyer is just good insurance against getting caught by a business technicality in a contract, lease or promissory note or running afoul of the labor laws. If you work closely with your lawyer, your chances of an adverse legal occurrence are diminished. Your lawyer can be your hero. Be wise in you lawyer selection. Too many lawyers are book smart and lack the streetwise nature of the business world. Too many lawyers are available to tell you what you cannot do, and too few lawyers are available to tell you what you can do to complete a transaction or properly run or expand your business.

Lawyers know why some people end up in litigation. They know how to keep you out of litigation. They can help you with entity choice, asset protection measures and succession planning.

Lawyers have specialties. Most lawyers can handle skillfully maybe two or three areas of the law. Beware of hiring a divorce lawyer to review your contracts, or worse yet represent you in a real estate deal. Before hiring, ask the lawyer what their specialties are. If they list more than three, run fast. Interview more than one lawyer, then hire the one with whom you have the best rapport and who is going to be your best team player. Labor law lawyers that are pro-business are a necessity to keep in contact with if you own a business.

Certified Public Accountant: CPAs have the experience of seeing the profits and losses of many businesses on a daily basis. CPAs should know how to make your business profitable and tell you about the pitfalls they have observed that make a business unprofitable. CPAs have different areas of focus: auditing, taxes, small business start-ups, management consulting and computer consulting. Find the CPA who is going to fill the void on your team.

The CPA should be willing to tell you frankly that your business is not going to make a million dollars the first year. Many young entrepreneurs are so full of excitement that they lose sight of reality. Sit with the CPA and prepare some realistic projections of the business. Authorize the CPA to prepare your projections and then authorize the CPA to prepare the CPA's projections of what the business might do.

Discuss the intimate details of your business with the CPA. CPAs are stereotypically introverts who love details and love numbers. Let them go to work for you.

Find a CPA who is a specialist in taxation. If you don't, up to 50% of your business profits could be contributed to the Treasury Department in the form of income taxes and Social Security taxes. You will want to invest money in your business in such a way that you minimize your income tax costs.

I remember talking to a group of businessmen in a small town, I was telling them about tax planning. They sullenly stared back as if this were something illegal.

In this day and age, all family financial plans should be assisted by a well-qualified tax specialist. The CPA is your money doctor. Go in for regular checkups.

There is a famous saying by Appeals Court Justice Learned Hand: "Every businessperson has the duty to themselves to arrange their financial affairs in such a way as to pay the least amount of tax possible under the law." Utilize this wisdom in all of your financial planning.

The CPA should be someone you can relate to and who can be a team player. This should be someone you feel comfortable with in discussing business strategies and parallel and congruent planning. There are many natural, normal, helpful and friendly CPAs out there. Your job is to find one.

Insurance Agent: Insurance companies are organized in such a way that your local representative may be either a representative of a large insurance company or a broker who can obtain insurance policies with a number of different companies.

Use your best judgment in this regard. It is much better to be represented by a name-brand company than to be insured by the First Fidelity Company of Mexico.

Always ask your insurance person about the A.M. Best or Standard and Poors rating of the company providing you with insurance coverage. Do not purchase a policy until you are convinced the company has a good chance of being around when you need them to pay you. Other rating services are Moody's Investor Services and Weiss Research. Do your homework.

Insurance people see countless business claims turned in to their company. They can tell you business war stories that are quite entertaining. Utilize this source of information.

Purchase the necessary insurance to cover the things your lawyer agrees you need to cover. Be sure policies don't overlap with one another so you don't pay for the same coverage twice.

Your insurance agent can be helpful by informing you how to cover your financial planning needs. Sit with your insurance person and learn from their wisdom. Take their recommendations to your lawyer and CPA. Learn from the team of professionals you have assembled to provide you with a strong financial future.

In order to start a business, you are going to need a team of professionals to help you get underway. Without assembling this resource network before you start your business, you are going to make your first bad business decision. You are going to increase your chances of failure.

Gain confidence in yourselves. Form a team approach to getting into business for yourself. Manage the effort in business as a unified team, focused on certain goals you want to achieve with your business.

Owning a business is not for everyone. Unless you have a strong sense of discipline, you will not fare very well as a self-employed person. Most self-employed people work 18 hours each day, 6 days per week, to get the business started.

There is a famous old saying among the self-employed that goes something like this: "I would rather work for myself eighteen hours per day so I don't have to work eight hours per day for someone else." Seasoned self-employed people really believe this. It has also been said that a bad day of fishing beats a great day at work!

There are countless sayings that point out the benefits of self-employment:

Either create your own journey or you'll become part of someone else's.

Don't hang out with the turkeys when you can break away and fly with the eagles.

You don't have to work hard for your money if you put your money to work hard for you.

Nothing in life is particularly hard if you divide the job into small steps.

Every person is as happy as they decide to be.

Once your business is beyond the five-year mark, you may be able to take 60 or 70 vacation days a year. Hard work, discipline, survival and endurance have their rewards.

Many people give self-employment a try. This is a very scary time for most of us, a time to get in touch with our fears and overcome them. We have many fears about starting our own business. These fears work against the possibility of success. You should try to harness and overcome your fears about self-employment and having your own business. Your fears are limiting the amount of financial success you can achieve.

In your own business you should see yourself as the president of the company, whether you are incorporated or not. See in your mind's eye that you are the president of your company. Each Monday, as well as every other day of the week, the time you spend working is based on your own decisions. Your old boss will not come around and tell you what to do.

In putting in your time on Monday, you can either work hard or you can work smart. If you work hard, you will probably earn about $8 per hour. If you work smart, you could earn $500 per hour. It's your choice.

An example of working hard versus working smart is a person named Joe who tried to start a cookie manufacturing company. Joe quit his job as an engineer with a Fortune 100 company. His mom had an outrageous cookie recipe, and he had a strong feeling the world would like the cookie as much as he did.

He rented some space in an industrial area. He spent quite a bit of money buying state-of-the-art machinery for the business. Joe was somewhat resourceful in buying the equipment, though: he bought most of it from various bakeries that had closed their doors. He made some conveyor belts and purchased some new bagging equipment.

Joe was very proud of his new business. For weeks he spent time rearranging the equipment to make the production area more speedy and efficient. When the equipment would break, Joe would be right there to fix it. Joe spent a lot of time in the production area.

After two years of business, Joe came to my office seeking consultation. He indicated that he thought he had a wonderful product. He spent 10 hours per day working in his business, but it did not seem to be making any money.

After two hours of analysis, I was able to put my finger on the problem. Joe was working hard in the business but not very smart. My analysis revealed that Joe's production area had the capacity to produce $2 million a year worth of product. Current sales were $100,000 per year.

As president of his company, Joe spent most of his time in the production area doing the work of a $25-per-hour, part-time machinery mechanic. He was busy and he worked hard. I redirected Joe to his office and had to almost chain him to the chair. I explained to Joe that there were two sides to his business: the production side and the marketing side. Joe barely could pronounce the word marketing. He asked for a more detailed explanation.

The president needs to manage the business. Joe needed to hire some people. First, he needed to hire a good marketing person that could establish distribution of the cookie in various market areas. Joe needed to hire a production manager who could work part-time as production manager and be trained to fix the machinery's minor problems. Then Joe could fix the machinery if there were major problems.

With this new management style, I had Joe plan out his week of work in advance. Each Friday before he could go home, he was to fill in a calendar, a daily planner, for the work he would do next week. Pulling Joe out of the production area and into the president's office was a very difficult task.

Joe followed the steps of the program. He was committed to seeing his company grow. Within six months, sales had soared. The orders came in. Reorders came in. New stores were ordering the product, and stores he had never contacted were calling the factory to get cookies delivered to them. Within one year, sales went from $100,000 to $800,000.

Joe was very happy. His new schedule required him to be at the factory four days a week. Some days he stayed for two hours and some days he worked ten hours. All of this was his choice.

From this, you can see the difference between working for someone else and working in your own business. There is no one around to tell you what to do. If you want to eat at the end of the month, you had better do something. If you work in the wrong direction, you will hold back the growth of your business. If you work in a direction that steadily improves sales and production, your business will grow. If you work your business as some sort of hourly clerk, there is no possible way to make a huge profit. If you work the business as the president of the company, you will start out working like an hourly clerk and soon grow to making huge profits.

Usually what holds the growth of a family-owned business back is the owner. Be aware of this. Plan your steps in advance. Talk the business over with your spouse, who can be a wonderful resource for seeing things you might miss. If you still have trouble getting the business off the ground, seek the services of a qualified business consultant who has a proven track record of knowing what to do to get a business to soar.

Joe's example shows what can happen with a manufacturing company, but the same problem of working in the wrong direction and holding back the growth of your business can occur in any self-employment situation. I have seen these same problems in law firms, doctors' offices, construction companies, retail stores and many other types of businesses. The important thing is not being the anchor that holds back the growth of your business.

Reflect upon the idea of starting a family-owned business to help you on your way to financial freedom. The family-owned business is one of the best tax shelters available under the United States tax code. Investigate the possibilities.

If you do not want to strike out to buy a family business, there are many ways you can work to succeed to the ownership position at the company where you are presently employed. There are many businesses out there that have owners who are older. One thing is for sure, these people will not live forever. They will either die early or reach an age when they have worked enough and want to enjoy life a little bit.

These business owners are always looking for qualified candidates to buy their businesses. You may want to make it your job to work hard and smart for your employer so they could one day trust the ownership of their business to you. Believe me, I have talked to many business owners who would be overjoyed to sell their business to a person who had worked hard for the business as a good, faithful, loyal and energetic employee.

Unfortunately, many times the employer feels that there is no qualified employee or group of employees that could successfully run the business in the future. The business owner needs a guarantee that they will be paid in full for the business when they retire. This usually requires monthly payments coming in from the successfully run business. This is why businesses usually sell to someone outside the company who is either financially fit to make the required payments or has a track record of hands-on, day-to-day management experience in running a company.

If you have an open and honest way of communicating with your employer, you can ask that employer to groom you to their satisfaction for taking over the business when they want to retire. Know where you stand in your business, and be sure you are working in the right direction with the right skills and motivation.

WHEN SELF-EMPLOYMENT IS NOT FOR YOU

Some people do not like owning a family business or working for smaller businesses, so consequently they have joined corporate America. These people have headed themselves in a direction to provide services to large corporations. Those who are on a professional track aspire to be a company department head or the president one day and command a huge salary with extra perks, bonuses and benefits. These people have to know how to climb the corporate ladder. They need to know how to work within the corporate organization and its politics. They need to work toward the top without looking like they are running a daily campaign for the office of president. If they do achieve the office of president, however, the world opens up to them. They are then sought after to be the president of other corporations if they do a successful job.

You need to know that a corporation is shaped like a pyramid, very wide at the bottom and very narrow at the top. The rank-and-file workers are represented at the bottom and the president at the top. The company may have 10,000 employees, but there is only one president. If you aspire to invest your career in corporate America, you must know that it gets very narrow at the top. As the field of upward mobility narrows, you either will remain at the same job in the same position or you will be laid off as others rise to the top, people who are better qualified or are better hooked into the team in power. You must know and study this environment and be able to work within the constraints of corporate structure.

In order to be president, you need to have in your arsenal an array of finely tuned job skills and people skills. You cannot mindlessly sit at your desk and hope that one day someone will come down the hall and ask you to be the president of the company. You need to work hard and smart in grooming yourself in business skills, marketing skills, personnel skills and motivational skills, and you need to have a keen sense of how your company earns a profit. You need to learn how to inexpensively create new products and product lines for your company. You need to take on the vision of a leader for the company, the captain of your boat. You have to gain the consent and support of your coworkers; you have to daily earn the job and title as president of the company. You cannot afford to have your company do poorly under your stewardship. If this happens, you might be ousted and never asked to be the president of any other company again.

Corporate life can be grueling, but it can provide an environment to help you build a strong financial future. Your career is made of choices that lead you and your family into prosperity. Whatever you choose, plan to work at your career with 110% of your effort.

INVESTING FOR FINANCIAL FREEDOM

Once you have chosen the career track that will gain you and your family financial freedom in the future, you will need to make investments from the profits of your work. In making investments, there are choices you need to make.

Your life is made up of your career, your family, your investments, and your spiritual, physical, mental and emotional needs.

In order to be financially successful, you cannot neglect to make investments. Many people find it hard to pronounce the word investments. You must quickly overcome this if this is your case. Once you are 25 years of age, you need to start your individual investment program. As the years go by, your financial responsibilities become greater, since you are not only investing for your individual needs but also for the needs of your spouse and children. You need to know and understand how to make investments. Having and managing investments is a very essential part of gaining your financial freedom.

Let's turn to the investment side of your life. In order to have financial freedom or retire, you will need to launch your career and make earnings and profits to roll into investments. This is the ageless process of creating wealth. Regardless of your occupation or career, you should plan to save from each pay period. You should put a minimum of 10% from each pay period into the investment side of your life. You should do this whether you are self-employed or employed by a company. Many opt for the employers 401(k) plan, some want to manage the investments themselves. Sometimes employers match the money you put into the company's pension plan.

SELECTING A STOCK BROKERAGE FIRM

To make investments in securities, it will be necessary to seek the services of a securities dealer of some kind. For stock investments most people select a stockbroker. They are trained professionals who can offer you investment advice, market reports and company research. They can tell you what the bigger individual investor accounts are buying.

There are many different alternatives in the marketplace. For larger sums of money there are professional portfolio managers to manage your account. There are full-service brokerage firms. There are discount brokerage firms. There are mutual fund companies that allow you to call an 800 telephone number direct to their office. There are firms like American Express that have more of a full-range financial planning service. There are insurance companies that offer some good advice in regard to financial planning and the positioning of your family's assets.

With so many professionals in the marketplace, how do you begin to pick and choose between them? Who will be a good investment manager to help you maintain control of your assets?

There are many professionals to lend you their opinion about how to invest your money. One thing you have to ask is why, if they are so good at making investments, are they still working and calling on you? What did they do with their money? What are their credentials for serving you in a safe and effective way?

You need to ask some very up-front and specific questions of any person who is going to lay their hands on your money. You might ask them how long they have been in business. What professional degrees do they have? What professional licenses do they possess, and what exactly are they qualified to do? Do they have an area of expertise or a specialty? What is their five-year and ten-year track record?

Can they refer you to a person who has been their client for more than two years and could say a good word about them?

You need to know the person's investment philosophy and approach to handling other people's money. You need to ask them their fees and fee structure. Before each transaction they conduct for you, you need to ask how much commission they are earning.

You need to know how much they are asking you to invest. Is there going to be a time when you need to put in more money to save your initial investment? How long will it take to get your principal back? Is there a chance you might lose any portion of the principal investment?

When will you be paid return on your investment? Is there a chance you will not be paid a return on your investment? For how many years is this investment likely to tie up your money?

You want the person to tell you all about risk. How much risk does this investment entail? Is this risk, in the professional's opinion, more risk than you should assume for your portfolio? Is there another investment you could make that would pay a similar return without assuming so much risk? Does this investment work into your individual, overall plan for diversification?

You want the person you select to evaluate your investment needs first. Then you need to discuss with the person the essentials of investing: risk management, diversification, a time line for expected return, income needs, appreciation or growth needs and foreign market investments.

You need to watch and monitor your investments. You need to subscribe to a financial newspaper that will allow you to do so. Many investors, for stock-watching purposes, subscribe to either The Wall Street Journal or to Investors Business Daily. These publications are readily available at your favorite newsstand. The publishers have special offers and discounted rates to first-time subscribers. Call them and ask for the special Money and Marriage discounted price. Tell them you read about them in this book.

Discount brokers publish their rates in these newspapers. Software companies oriented to stock investments also advertise in these newspapers. By reading these publications, you will find investment tools helpful to you and your needs.

When you make investments in companies, you will need to conduct your own tracking research that keeps you informed, first hand, as to the present status and market value of the shares you own.

Some companies available for investment will show prospect of gain in the future because they are positioned to grow. How you select which companies or mutual funds to invest in is a result of your research. You must conduct some evaluation of your own personal investment goals and objectives.

Stock investments pay you in two basic ways. They pay you dividends. Dividends are your earnings for making stock investments. This is sometimes compared to the interest you earn at a bank. The other way stock investments pay you is when the stock appreciates. The stock appreciates when the value of the stock goes up. If your stock pays you

3% annual dividend and grows 12% for the year in stock value, then you have earned the equivalent of 15% return on the investment for the year.

Above is a very basic way to look at stock investments. If you invest in a mutual fund company, you will have a little less homework because you will not have to track the investment as closely as you would when you invest directly in a stock. This all may seem new and complicated when you first look at it. One thing you need to know, though: in order to retire you must learn about investments. It is best to learn at age 25 and thus be a 40-year pro at making investments when you reach age 65. Or you can wait and begin learning about investments when you reach age 65. It is your choice. Most people, anxious to gain their financial freedom, would like to learn about investments at age 25 and then be a seasoned pro when it is time to invest for their retirement.

Some growth stock companies or growth stock mutual funds will not pay you a dividend at all. Some companies that are going to grow slowly will pay you a monthly or quarterly dividend. Some companies that pay a dividend are set up to allow you to reinvest that dividend in that company's stock. This arrangement is called a dividend reinvestment plan.

If you invest in a company that has a dividend reinvestment plan, you can purchase more shares in that company without paying a commission at all. Dividend reinvestment plans are made available by companies that allow your dividend earnings to be reinvested in additional shares of stock. To make your investment grow bigger with that company, you might want to take part in the company's dividend reinvestment plan.

Brokerage firms offer margin accounts. Margin accounts are arrangements that allow you to post as collateral the existing shares of stock you own in many companies. The brokerage firm will extend you credit and allow you to purchase even more shares than you already have without contributing any more money. This is very risky, and I do not recommend margin accounts to beginning and novice investors. Those who have been in the market and are more sophisticated investors are expertly able to use margin accounts to their financial advantage. There are too many stories of people who have been away from their telephone on vacation and come home to find out that the brokerage firm called in the margin account and sold all of the collateral. Your stock investments could turn to ashes if this were to happen.

Whenever you place an order with a person selling securities, you want to follow up your conversation with a written memo of exactly what your instructions were. This memo should be precise in listing the terms, conditions, quantities, dates, prices, limitations and all special instructions for your order. You may want to e-mail this memo. You may want to send this memo by mail with return receipt requested. It is very important to write down your trade instructions the same day and mail a memo of those instructions to the person who is going to make the investment or trade for you. You will want to cover any special instructions you have given the trader in your written memo.

When you place an order for a common stock, it is very interesting what happens. Not many people have visited the behind-the-scenes activity. The summary of what happens is something like this. Your broker places your order into the branch office computer. That order goes to headquarters or directly onto the floor of the stock exchange. The firm you placed the order with has a representative on the floor of the exchange. This representative is wired via computer and receives a copy of your order. He places the order with a specialist on the floor of the exchange who is trading the stock you requested. The trade is then executed at an agreed price. A confirmation of the order then comes back to your local branch office after the order on the floor of the exchange is completed. This whole process takes place in a short period of time. When you visit the floor of the exchange, you can see a lot of people moving briskly, keeping up with the orders that are pouring in.

Some people ask if they should get the stock certificate of the company stock they just purchased or leave the stock holdings in the brokerage account. If the broker holds the stock, this is referred to as holding the stock in street name. Holding stock in street name will be much more convenient when you want to sell the stock or a portion of the stock. If you hold the certificate, you will have to go to your safe deposit box, get the certificate, drive it to the brokerage firm and go through some paperwork to complete the delivery of the shares to the brokerage firm. A lot of time running around can be saved by holding stock in street name at the brokerage firm. This can get more complicated if you want to sell only a portion of the shares or if your stock has split, merged or provided some other benefit to you. The itemized monthly statement your brokerage firm gives you will provide the details about and evidence of what stock you have.

Let's talk commissions and fees. Your securities dealer will charge either a commission or a fee, but not both. If they are charging a commission, sometimes they charge a commission up front, when you buy, and at the end, when you sell. The commission can be from waived (or zero) up to 5%. You need to ask what the commission is and then weigh it against the professional services offered, the research materials offered and the assistance you receive with the management and positioning of your financial assets. The more useful help they offer, the more interested you should be in paying a commission. Most commissions are negotiable because salespeople make their money each time they can talk you into buying. Then they make money each time they can talk you into selling. You can see that if their money comes in each time you buy and each time you sell, they do not have any incentive to see you make a profit in the transaction. They are only interested in having you trade in a buy or sell transaction, since this is how their money comes to them. They are not paid any more or any less if you make a profit in the transaction.

Some brokers have been unscrupulous in this regard. For example, they might call and tell you that some company has just gotten an FDA approval or has begun expanding into adjoining states. They make the case that you have to buy this stock right now, immediately, with no time to spare. Then in a month they call you back and tell you that something terrible is going to happen with the company they just recommended and you should sell, that there is little time to spare because another company looks more promising. After this transaction is complete, they let a few months go by before contacting you again and suggesting you sell that stock and invest in another. This is the basic scenario of "churning the account," which is illegal. The more blue your hair and the more you look like a grandmother, the better chance you have of successfully recovering from the firm the commissions and investment losses incurred in such a situation. You should avoid a broker who is going to churn your account.

If you want to buy a small number of shares in a company, you are going to pay a higher commission than if you purchase 100 shares or more. In brokerage terminology an order of less than 100 shares is an "odd lot" order. You can still place the order and test the integrity of your broker at the same time. The broker should tell you that the order you are placing is an odd lot order and they are going to have to charge you a higher commission than normal.

As you become more familiar with brokerage firm investments and the different ways of making investments, you will learn that, just like rolling the dice in Las Vegas, there are many different ways to cover your investment in a stock.

When you call your broker, you can ask to place your investment in a particular stock in such a way that you make money if the stock goes up. You can also place your investment in a particular stock in such a way that you make money if that stock goes down. It is up to you to predict which direction the stock price of that company will go. When you have an idea of the direction of the stock price for that company, call your broker and place an order. Remember, you can place an order and invest money with the hope that a stock will go down. If that stock goes down, you make money. You can place an order and invest money with the hope that a stock will go up. If that stock goes up, you make money.

Sometime, just for fun, I have asked friends to call me when they buy a stock hoping it will go up. What I do is buy the same stock with the hope that it goes down. Sometimes when investors do not do their homework they make investments at the wrong time and the stock goes off in the wrong direction. I really enjoy calling a buddy when his stock goes down and thanking him in a friendly, way for the good tip, because I watched what happened and know he lost money on the investment. On that same investment I was able to make money by betting the other way.

If you want to gain more insight into buying common stocks, you should purchase Peter Lynch's "One Up On Wall Street." Peter provides some great insight into how simple it can be to pick stocks, make the right investment decisions and make a profit in common stocks.

SELECTING A FINANCIAL PLANNER

Part of planning to gain your financial freedom requires that you meet with a skilled financial planner. Again, it is better to meet the financial planner when you are age 25 to learn sound ideas and concepts. It is very difficult to learn all you must know when you first look into financial planning at age 65.

Be careful! There are all types of people out there posing as financial planners. You need to carefully select and investigate the financial planner you propose to use. You need to visit with at least two financial planners. You need to make inquiries of them the same way you did when selecting your stockbroker. You need to be aware that for almost everything you buy from a financial planner, the financial planner is earning a commission.

Always ask what that commission will be. Never buy life insurance or disability insurance from a stand-alone financial planner. If you have selected a large, quality firm that does structured financial planning and also sells life insurance, this is all right. Make sure the company is the size of American Express or larger before you buy life insurance from the financial planner.

Some financial planners charge hourly fees. This is sometimes all right. Make sure you have a firm understanding of how you are going to be charged, when are you going to be charged and when the fee is due to your financial planner. Yes, financial planning fees are deductible on your federal tax return.

Be alert when working with a financial planner. No one is going to be more careful and watchful of your money than you are. Be sure you are aware at all times of what is happening with your money. Never expect that your money is going to triple in size unwatched or unmanaged by yourself. The financial planner is an advisor only. You need to take charge of and manage your own life, money and investments. The financial planner can offer ideas and guidance as to what you can do with your money. Do not place false hope in your financial advisors to effectively and efficiently invest your money. Only you can prevent investment mistakes.

The financial planner should be equipped to look at your total financial position. The stockbroker typically will only help you invest a specific sum of money, which you give to them. Thus, the financial planner's first job is to get an idea of what your financial picture looks like right now. If you need credit counseling, do not look to a financial planner to provide you with credit counseling assistance. Thank your financial planner for recommending a credit counseling firm that can help you with your needs.

While getting old debt taken care of and getting you onto the right financial track, the financial planner can continue to evaluate and measure your total financial picture. Your financial planner can help you position your assets so you have balance in your financial future. Your financial planner then needs to evaluate your specific needs, goals and objectives. The financial planner will point out what tools, investments and products will help you get there.

It is sad that many financial planners are not skilled enough to really help you. Be sure you have carefully interviewed and screened your financial planner. Be sure you have talked face-to-face with at least three satisfied customers of the financial planner. Be certain these satisfied customers know exactly what the return on their investments has been, and ask them how effectively the financial planner helped with positioning the assets to help them meet their financial goals.

Most certified financial planners got their certificate by mail order. Just about anyone who pays the fees and takes a course can become a certified financial planner and join an organization of national financial planners.

You will find in the long run that it is best to purchase stock from a stockbroker, life insurance from a life insurance company, financial planning ideas from a qualified financial planner, banking services from a bank, tax advice from a skilled tax specialist who is a CPA and legal advice from a lawyer. This paragraph of advice may save you a lifetime of heartache.

Your financial freedom will come from properly managing the time you invest in your career. The normal work week is made up of eight hours per day, five days per week. This is 40 hours per week for 52 weeks, which totals 2,080 hours per year that you channel into your career. With the proceeds of your career, you will channel no less than 10% of your earnings into investments that are designed to provide for your financial future, college planning needs and the financial needs of your family for the generations to follow. You retire when you have channeled enough career earnings into investments to receive sufficient financial yield to meet your daily, weekly and annual living expenses. You should work hard together with your spouse to gain your financial freedom.

The decision to retire depends on achieving financial freedom and having a sufficient income to cover living expenses comfortably. Financial freedom means having saved enough to maintain your desired lifestyle without relying on employment income. Before retiring, assess your savings, investments, and retirement accounts to ensure they can sustain your lifestyle for decades. Calculate your expected retirement expenses, including healthcare and unforeseen costs, and compare them to your projected income from retirement accounts, pensions, and social security. A rule of thumb is that your retirement income should replace at least 70-80% of your pre-retirement income. Additionally, consider your health, desired retirement activities, and personal goals. Once you've achieved financial security and are ready to embrace a lifestyle that suits you, it may be time to retire. Regularly review your financial plan to adapt to changing circumstances throughout retirement.

The people that I have met in the golf course that are comfortably retired in resort communities have these sources of income insuring their permanent retirement. Either they have real estate units that they collect rent from or the had developed a successful business that sold for more than $100 million dollars. There is clue to the wise here.

MANTRA

I will do whatever is necessary to gain my financial freedom.

CHAPTER 6

Open Your Heart to Finances

There are many romantic things a married couple can do together, but managing the household finances is not often one of the activities listed on that list. For some couples managing finances has been a romantic thing to do. Consequently, they have enjoyed great financial success. Teaming together is a helpful component of amassing great wealth. Teamwork is much better than one person amassing wealth and then having to set strategies to protect that wealth by keeping the other spouse out of the household financial planning picture. The *teamwork strategy* is much more fun than the *protection and preservation strategy*. Teamwork will make your relationship more rewarding, fulfilling and complete. The protection and preservation strategies were very prevalent in the 1940s and 1950s, and they are still in vogue today if you spouse has other talents and this whole net worth building thing, is not their thing. They would much rather spend their time shopping and going to the spa or playing sports and going to the bar. To be able to build your net worth you have to establish some common ground and a mode to deal with the finances of your married household. Before this book some couples fought like cats and dogs for the first five years of marriage and then finally worked out a money system for their household and they don't want anyone to mess with it!

Money management requires holding on to, summarizing, evaluating and analyzing important financial records and documents. Money management requires attention to details. You must have these skills in your personal arsenal. If you do not have them, do your best soul-searching to find them within yourself and use them to the best of your ability.

Balancing the family checkbook is a dreaded chore; it is something that's still not taught in our high schools with any great depth. A family unit usually chooses one person to be the financial representative of the family. This is the person who pays the bills, balances the checkbook and categorizes all the household expenditures into preselected categories for easy review at the end of each month. There are computer programs that help with this task. There are check registers you can purchase at an office supply store to help you categorize the actual monthly household expenditures in check number order. You can choose to do it by hand or you can choose to use technology.

In deciding who in the family will be the financial representative, many winning strategies have worked. Please take note that extremely artistic, creative people sometimes develop a very real fear of numbers and details. Attention to detail does not come easy for these people. Understand that your spouse may not have the same level of passion for and control of financial details as you do. You should take this into consideration when electing the family document controller, office manager and record keeper (vice president of finance).

I counseled a family that tried to save money in business by hiring the wife to keep the books. (Normally the husband was the worker and the wife was the homemaker.) The wife gave bookkeeping a gallant effort, but just could not seem to grasp the concepts needed to keep things straight. After a little study, we learned that she was highly creative and artistic. Her projects in the home were fantastic and beautiful. She was highly oriented toward creativity. She lacked those components for adding up columns of numbers and making sense of minute details. She was not kidding when she would sigh and say that bookkeeping was not her thing. At first the husband began complaining and telling the wife about how hard he worked, asking why she couldn't do the simple office tasks that would only take a normal person an hour or two per day. This led to conflict between the spouses. Once they both learned what the problem was, the wife was relieved of bookkeeping and put in charge of marketing for the company, which soon she became quite successful.

Do not take lightly the fact that some highly creative people are not mentally geared to take on the details required for good record keeping.

Someone needs to be appointed to the task. If you cannot find a volunteer between you, hire someone. It may cost a little money, but it may save you hours of frustration.

You need to discover together the components of your overall financial makeup.

THE MAKEUP OF YOUR FINANCIAL LIFE

In order to focus your energy on net worth building, you must discover that you really can manage money and amass wealth. Anyone who puts their mind and focused energy to this task can accomplish increases in their financial net worth. Many people fear they cannot, and the rest are too lazy to do it.

Your financial life is made up of three prongs:

1. Your career. This is your job, how you have elected to earn your money. From this job you earn your salary, your take-home pay, or drawings from your family business. Regardless of the form it takes, this is your source of earnings and new capital.

2. Your personal life. This is your home life, the time you spend with family, self and spouse. You need to break away from your office/job behavior when you are around the house. Many books about leaving the office behind suggest that you have a halfway destination after work where you can gather yourself and make the transition from work life to home life. This will enable you to begin shortly after work to participate in a meaningful and fulfilling way in your home life. For some the gym has become the place to accomplish this. No, this does not authorize stopping for a drink after work. Drinking before transforming into your home life mode and behavior can cause you to treat family members in a bad way. Some people have tried to come home and lock themselves in their room while they exercise or meditate after a long workday. This causes problems because you require your loved ones to keep their distance at a time when they are most enthusiastic about greeting you and interacting with you.

    Find a gym, library, swimming pool, tennis court or some transition place, if you need this. This will enable you to make a smooth transition from your work life to your home life.

3. Your investment life. This is the place to begin your net worth building. A percentage of your earnings are placed into selected

investments to help you reap capital appreciation in the future. You must become awakened to your investment life. Some people are not aware that their investment life exists.

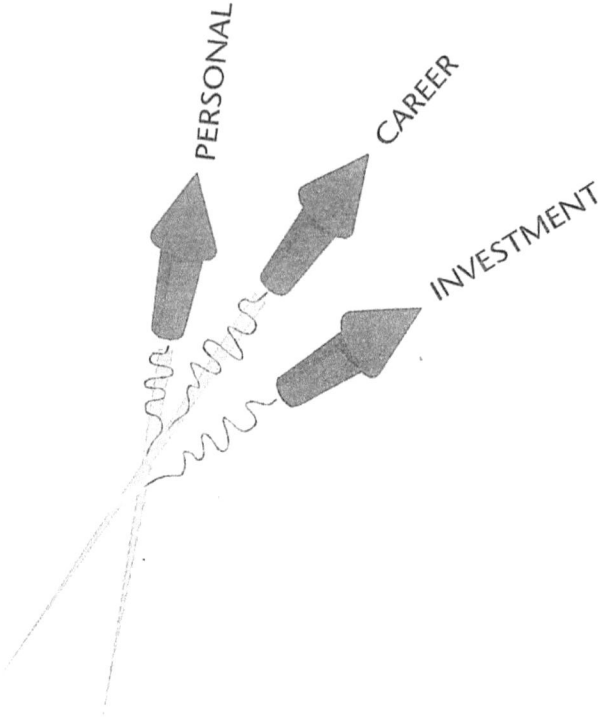

BALANCING YOUR LIFE

To ensure a good relationship with your spouse and family members, you must balance your career and home life. You cannot avoid home life and bury yourself in your career in the name of building finances, as many people do.

With these three arenas of career, personal life and investments to manage, you must learn to balance your time appropriately between them. Balance is the key that I suggest to my clients. You must continually balance these three arenas.

If any one of these parts goes out of commission or takes a downturn, it will affect your emotional, mental and physical state. When a person is out of kilter, they are probably not providing a loving, supportive, creative environment for their partner or their children.

Without balance, you will spend too much time working and not enough time at home with your family or your spouse. Many highly paid executives avoid the stress of child-rearing by busying themselves at the office. There is always a reason they are not available on the weekends or after five o'clock for family.

You cannot put all your time into family, because you would not have much in the way of earnings.

You cannot put all your time into your career, because you would not have much in the way of family.

You cannot put all of your earnings into investments, since that would leave no room for a reasonable and comfortable lifestyle.

A reasonable and comfortable lifestyle is what a balanced family would have. Keeping up with the neighbors and needing to be one up on your peers are destructive to increasing your net worth. For your household, reasonable and comfortable may mean living on 80% of your annual earnings and investing 20%, for other households the percentages will vary. In order to accomplish positive net worth building progress, however, these percentages should not vary by much.

Prudent, rational, reasonable, responsible, disciplined people would not obligate their household to more than 80% of their net take-home pay.

This is very reasonable, but in over 20 years in my financial planning practice I have met very few new clients who have actually done this. I could easily say that fewer than 5% of all of my new clients have done this. Startling, isn't it?

When you consider your net take-home pay and your spending practices, and then consider the idea of spending no more than 80% of your net take-home pay, you need to consider family emergencies, college education, periods of unemployment and aging parents. These are the top categories that will throw you off course in maintaining a practice of 20% of your earnings going into investments.

Additionally, you are wanting to create a home for your spouse and children. Your home does not have to be large or expensive. It does need to be a safe haven and a refuge for each family member. You need to work at creating this. Happiness in the home comes from being available and sharing activities, love, hugs, nurturing and affection, not from bricks, mortar and swimming pools.

The home is a platform for love and exuberance, positive praise and direction. The home is your palace of pleasure. Great pains should be taken to have fun, laughter and crazy good times at home. The home is the springboard of creativity.

The home is where the physical, mental and emotional needs of the child develop. Your child will be constantly recording what is said and done in the home environment. Much of what you do could scar your child, and this will be manifested in later life, traditionally when your child reaches their late thirties and early forties.

It is surprising how much love and exuberance flows from parents, thus creating a happy and healthy atmosphere, when their financial affairs are in order. This comes from living within your financial means.

For the child, you need to create boundaries and discipline while rewarding success. Set them up to succeed at every task, then celebrate their success with them. Catch them if they fall, prop them up, then help them see the way to succeed. Provide them with reassurance of your continued availability to help. Let them think it through themselves, help them develop their own successful thought patterns. Help them find a way to link success into their life. If you do, you will be helping your children on the path of net worth building, since these are the tools needed by every individual. The earlier you can get started, the better.

One great family investment idea that included the children was a family that bought each child an investment property, a fourplex, when the child reached age 10. They guided the children in the duties and responsibilities of managing the property and collecting the rents. The children learned about repairs, paying bills and managing a mortgage. The children learned that if the units stayed full there was a profit. Some of the profit went toward college savings, some of it was used for their spending money. This arrangement worked very well for the family. The children grew up to be very successful business people.

The home is the incubator for your child's developmental behavior, through reaching, exploring, asserting, competing, caring, sympathizing, loving and integrating. They also learn to be responsible to self, their future partner and society.

This occurs throughout the stages of childhood: attachment, exploration, identity, competence, concern and intimacy.

A child will go a lot farther if they are constantly reminded that they can be successful instead of constantly being put down and told what a no good such-and-such they are going to be when they grow up. They will have to spend some time with a therapist in their late thirties to get rid of this negative programming in their subconscious minds.

Another destructive part of dealing with the household finances is the situation where there are two busy parents who both put too much time into their careers and not enough time into the household. This also can occur when there is a single working parent household. Often in these cases parents indulge the children with material things in an attempt to put a fix on not being there after school or at school plays, sporting events or amusement park outings, whatever the activity the parent feels guilty about. The parent buys the child too many toys or other material things to make up for this or hires someone to take the child to a movie, play or sporting event. This is the wrong road to take. You are not helping the child at all. You are probably making yourself feel good. You are not having the natural feeling of guilt that you should have for conducting yourself in such a way. You are masking your personal guilt. This is all that is being accomplished. You are not helping your child, who is a person of many needs, all of which require your personal time, attention and attendance.

Your child needs your time.

Children are designed to be nurtured. If you want them to be financially successful, nurture them to the fullest. Build their pride, self-esteem and self-confidence. There are no shortcuts to parenting. The child needs you to be there for a balanced number of activities. The child needs your presence, your praise and emotional warmth throughout the development years. Every child needs physical and emotional contact. A child needs a reliable source of love and comfort.

Acquiring a stream of material things is only setting the child up for problems in the future, including problems in their marriage relationship.

If you find wealth building difficult for yourself, reflect back on your childhood and identify what was missing so you can begin the healing process and get underway developing your individual financial assets. Quite likely there is something present today from your childhood that is limiting or preventing you from breaking away from the pack and becoming a champion net worth builder.

If you feel you cannot develop substantial net worth, I can begin to identify the things in your development years that are presently creating the roadblock to your financial success.

You do not have to be brought up in the perfect household in order to succeed. You do, however, need to get in touch with what was left out and heal from that oversight on the part of your parents in grooming successful offspring.

There are many success stories about children who had terrible childhood experiences. There are many failures of daddy's/mommy's spoiled little brat.

This book is calling to your attention that the roots of your romantic relationship are within your childhood experiences. You must grow and adjust in order to commence the process of building your financial net worth. In order to do this, you must identify and heal your childhood wounds.

An important ingredient of the ideal relationship is finding a partner who is a match in your desires to build a strong financial future. Who you choose is such an important part in starting your romantic and financial future. Find a partner with a similar family background and the same morals and values as you. A good lifetime match does not come from marrying the wild and crazy thing you met swinging from the rafters in a bar.

Much like you have committed to a lifetime relationship, you must commit to a lifetime of conserving, managing and growing financial assets. There is a ceremony that acknowledges the commitment to the relationship; there should be a bigger ceremony and celebration that acknowledges the commitment to the building of a strong financial future.

After agreeing on a financial plan, couples should celebrate, in some commemorative and memorable way, the commitment they have made to each other to work mutually toward the building of financial assets.

MANAGING YOUR PAYCHECK

If you derive your earnings from a paycheck, you need to understand some of the basic components and behind-the-scenes details.

In your paycheck, you receive your gross pay less a number of off-sets or amounts withheld. The withholding is made up of several components. One of the components is your Social Security withholding. If you have had more than one employer during any one calendar year, you might be eligible for a refund of overpaid Social Security amounts on your income tax return.

Another component of withholding is your federal income tax withholding. These are the monies that are taken and deposited into an account bearing your Social Security number at the Internal Revenue Service. You are not paid interest on these monies. The money rests there until you file your annual income tax return. When you specify the amount of tax you owe on your return, this is then compared to what you have already paid into your account. The difference, if any, is paid to you as a refund. The amount of money withheld is determined by the information you record on the FORM W-4 you placed with your employer when you started working for the company. You can adjust the FORM W-4 any time during your work year, and you can change it back when you need to. Your company's payroll department is available to give to you a new FORM W-4 when you need one.

Too often I hear that people have filed their income tax return and they "made money" that year, meaning they received a refund, let's say $800. This may occur if you paid in $12,000 in withholding and your tax was only $11,200. This would entitle you to a refund of $800. You did not make any money. Your family lost $11,200 of its wealth-building capability.

Receiving a refund is no indication that you "made money" or not. You may get a refund after you have paid several thousand dollars in tax. The refund is only the settling process. If you carefully look at your tax return, you will see you paid several thousand dollars in income tax. Your objective should be to place your investments in such a way as to minimize this cost each year. If you receive a refund, you are only getting back some of the income tax you already paid into the system. The money is withheld. You never get to handle, touch or see the money. Then all of a sudden you get some of it back. Do not confuse this process with making money.

Another type of withholding is for charitable contributions you may have authorized at work. If you have charitable withholding, you should make a note of the amount so you receive full credit for the amount paid when it is time to do your income tax return at the end of the year.

The end result on your paycheck is a component of earnings called "net take-home pay." This is a very important number. All of your household financial planning steps should be done by using and making reference to the net take-home pay. Too many households consciously know what they have agreed to with the employer as their gross pay. Then they gear all of their spending based upon the gross pay. This leads to financial disaster.

You need to base all of your annual spending and investment plans on your net take-home pay.

If this principle is learned at a very early age, you will undoubtedly save yourself years of frustration. Too many people base their spending upon gross pay. Too many people are locked into a syndrome of living beyond their paycheck. You need to have a money management system in your household. The system must track the amount of net take-home pay on a monthly basis. This system must track actual spending.

The actual spending needs to be compared monthly to your money game plan for the year. The money game plan for the year is your budget. You need to track and categorize actual spending, compare it to budgeted spending and note the differences. Without a tracking system, you will never know how you are actually doing. This would be as much a disaster as running a company without looking at the company's financial statements to help you make management decisions.

The following is a helpful guide to classifying your spending. You need to know if your spending is done daily, monthly or annually. For example, the registration on your car is due annually. Birthdays for the children are annual, but depending on the number of children you have, they could be monthly! Mortgage payments are due monthly. Costs for lunch are daily. You need to formulate a master chart. Something that might be helpful is using an old calendar with big squares so you can write into the squares the known payments.

Chart out the whole year. Naturally, your household is not going to have the exact same spending each month of the year. You need to chart out the whole year so you can provide for extra money in the months that extra high costs are going to occur. Thus, you will have planned spending for birthdays, vacation, anniversaries, Christmas and other items that are not reoccurring each month.

You want to plan each month to fund some money toward a small savings account entitled "Emergencies." Having an emergencies saving account funded monthly will allow you to survive emergencies without fouling your monthly spending plans.

You need to develop a tracking system to track your checks issued, new charges to your credit cards, and amounts withdrawn from the bank by way of checks to cash or raids on the ATM machine. Never deposit your paycheck and ask for cash back in the same transaction. You should have a planned amount per week or per month for pocket money. Write a check and cash it. This will help you in your tracking system. Buy a writing tablet at the stationery store or purchase some inexpensive software at the computer store to help you with your tracking efforts or simply use Excel.

Once you have tracked the money, fill in the monthly report that appears on the following pages.

MONTHLY SPENDING PLAN

	Actual Spending	Planned Spending	Variance
INVESTMENT (Number One Item)			
Monthly savings	_____	_____	_____
College tuition	_____	_____	_____
Mutual fund	_____	_____	_____
Common stock	_____	_____	_____
Real estate	_____	_____	_____
IRA account-01	_____	_____	_____
IRA account-02	_____	_____	_____

Emergency fund   _____   _____   _____
Mortgage backup saving   _____   _____   _____

FOOD:

Grocery   _____   _____   _____
Lunch adults   _____   _____   _____
Lunch children   _____   _____   _____

HOUSING:

Mortgage   _____   _____   _____
Utilities   _____   _____   _____
Telephone   _____   _____   _____
Cable TV   _____   _____   _____
Taxes   _____   _____   _____
Insurance   _____   _____   _____
Landscaping   _____   _____   _____
Repairs   _____   _____   _____
Improvements   _____   _____   _____

CLOTHES:

Husband   _____   _____   _____
Wife   _____   _____   _____
Child-01   _____   _____   _____
Child-02   _____   _____   _____

MERCANTILE:

Household supplies   _____   _____   _____
Kitchen equipment   _____   _____   _____
Cleaning supplies   _____   _____   _____
Furniture   _____   _____   _____
Furnishings & decor   _____   _____   _____

ENTERTAINMENT:

Restaurants in town   _____ _____ _____
Restaurants while traveling _____ _____ _____
Theater   _____ _____ _____
Sporting events   _____ _____ _____
Lodging   _____ _____ _____
Airfare   _____ _____ _____
Sporting equipment   _____ _____ _____
Vacations   _____ _____ _____
Exercise   _____ _____ _____
Other entertainment: _____ _____ _____
_____   _____ _____ _____

MEDICAL & HEALTH:

Husband   _____ _____ _____
Wife   _____ _____ _____
Child-01   _____ _____ _____
Child-02   _____ _____ _____
Other medical: _____ _____ _____
_____ _____ _____ _____

INSURANCE:

Auto   _____ _____ _____
Health   _____ _____ _____
Home   _____ _____ _____
Life   _____ _____ _____
Umbrella coverage   _____ _____ _____
Extended coverage   _____ _____ _____

TRANSPORTATION:

Payments/Lease auto-01   _____ _____ _____
Payments/Lease auto-02   _____ _____ _____

Gasoline   _____ _____ _____
Washes   _____ _____ _____
Repair   _____ _____ _____
Tires   _____ _____ _____
Registration   _____ _____ _____
Parking fees & meters _____ _____ _____
Tickets   _____ _____ _____
Subway & trains   _____ _____ _____
Taxi & tips   _____ _____ _____
Other: _____ _____ _____
_____ _____ _____ _____

HOUSEHOLD DEBT:

Credit card-01   _____ _____ _____
Credit card-02   _____ _____ _____
Student loans   _____ _____ _____
College tuition   _____ _____ _____

CHILDREN:

Kiddie equipment _____ _____ _____
Education   _____ _____ _____
Child care   _____ _____ _____
Toys   _____ _____ _____

GIFTS:

Anniversary   _____ _____ _____
Birthday-01   _____ _____ _____
Birthday-02   _____ _____ _____
Birthday-03   _____ _____ _____
Birthday-04   _____ _____ _____
Grandma   _____ _____ _____
Grandpa   _____ _____ _____

Christmas   _____ _____ _____
Charities   _____ _____ _____
Church   _____ _____ _____
Other gifts: _____ _____ _____

_____   _____ _____ _____

OTHER COSTS:

Household help   _____ _____ _____
Clubs   _____ _____ _____
Organizations   _____ _____ _____
Newspapers   _____ _____ _____
Magazines   _____ _____ _____
Computer equipment   _____ _____ _____
Computer software   _____ _____ _____
Computer games   _____ _____ _____
Computer supplies   _____ _____ _____
Computer telephone   _____ _____ _____
Computer educational   _____ _____ _____
Hair care   _____ _____ _____
Body care   _____ _____ _____
Pets   _____ _____ _____
Hobbies   _____ _____ _____
Dry cleaning   _____ _____ _____
Other: _____ _____ _____

_____   _____ _____ _____

_____   _____ _____ _____

_____   _____ _____ _____

This list is designed to give you ideas. You should eliminate the line items that do not pertain to your household and add items that are required for your household. On a monthly basis, you should prepare a summary of actual spending, prepare a summary of planned spending (your budget), and mathematically compute the variances. By studying the variances, you will know whether you are ahead of the spending plan for the month (reflecting a favorable variance) or off course in your planned spending (reflecting an unfavorable variance).

To adopt a budget for your household takes mutual understanding of each other's needs, priorities, wants, dreams and desires. You need to be good communicators. You need to practice your communication skills in all aspects of your daily life. You need to put to use your effective communication skills in adopting and managing your household budget and finances.

Regardless of your monthly income, you need to track, monitor and manage your household finances by completing a monthly report that provides you, as managers, the necessary information and feedback you need to see how you are doing.

If you are not presently making a written monthly financial report, you have developed a fundamental bad habit. Bad habits are easy to break if you know the process. You need to clearly define the habit you want to replace. Identify the new habit you want to have. Line up your core beliefs and feelings with your new habit and begin doing it. Follow these steps, and you can change any behavior.

Get the point? Preparing this monthly financial report is essential and necessary for every household. No one is exempt.

Now make an annual list similar to this monthly list for charting your annual spending. You can modify and use this list by providing a column for each month in the year. The next section tells you how to make a list like this for the year.

CREATING YOUR ANNUAL SPENDING PLAN WORKSHEET

Step 1
Use the same categories as provided in the left-hand margin of the monthly spending plan.

Step 2
Across the top of the page, make a column for each month in the year.

Step 3

Title the last column "YTD Total" (year-to-date total). You thus need at least 13 columns across for numbers.

Step 4

With the old calendar you used for writing in your annual commitments, prepare an annual spending plan. Fill in the appropriate amounts for each month of the year. Insert your fixed monthly costs, i.e., rent, auto payments, medical costs, utilities, etc. Next insert those monthly variable costs for birthdays, Christmas, vacations, semiannual payments of registration, taxes, premiums for insurance, etc. Enter them in the column of the appropriate month.

Step 5

Add the columns down to arrive at the monthly projected spending totals. Add the rows across to arrive at the year's projected cost totals for each category.

There is a reason and purpose of doing this work. The purpose is to get away from the habit of the cycle of earn and spend. If you aimlessly earn and spend you eventually wake up deep in dept with no contributions towards investments which lead to building you financial net worth.

With the above worksheet you have created your annual spending plan. Each January you should adopt a new annual spending plan. With the numbers on the annual spending plan, you can fill in the monthly planned spending column on your monthly planned spending worksheet. The column on your monthly report entitled "Planned Spending" comes from what you have entered on your annual spending plan worksheet.

The very next time you see your spouse after reading this portion of the book, tell them you are committed to preparing an annual spending plan and a monthly spending plan for charting and tracking household expenses.

Renew this commitment with your spouse each year. Take the time to elect which person is going to do the work of tracking and charting the monthly household expenses. This should be considered a household chore, just like vacuuming the carpet. While the carpet gets vacuumed in most households, categorizing, charting and tracking monthly expenses is done in few households. This charting and tracking is essential for your overall financial health. Commit to having a financially healthy household.

Too many households run on free-wheeling and spending without tracking or feedback. By having a tracking system that provides you with feedback, it is much harder to spend beyond your means.

Each month you need to know if you are on track for the year. If you aren't, then you will know that spending needs to be curtailed. If you are on track, everything is fine and you can splurge on that new toy.

If I could tell you one thing and one thing only about managing your paycheck, it would be to write the first check every month to your investment account. Commit to a percentage of your net take-home pay that will go to savings. By writing the first check every month to your own investment account, your investment fund will have money in it. If, like most people, you plan to write a check to your investment account each month but always seem to run out of money before you get around to it, your investment account will never get funded. I have seen people carry the idea of funding their investment account for five years before they agreed to write the investment check first. Then all of a sudden, they get on track and are forever glad they learned this vital technique.

By first writing a check to your investment account after receiving your paycheck every pay period, you will magically have money going toward investments each month. You will still struggle to make ends meet each month, but the dryness in your checking account delivers you the signal to curtail spending. Your household financial reports should deliver you this same message in a clearer way. If you insist on not preparing monthly household financial reports, your household will become another one that is financially mismanaged. Do not allow your household, your family or your future to become financially mismanaged. Take those positive steps to a bright financial future. I always get suspicious of the spouse in counseling sessions who makes the case for not wanting to prepare the monthly financial report. Who are they kidding? What are they hiding? These are the questions I have as their financial counselor. What is their real adgenda?

You do not need to conduct a life of deprivation. I am floored by families that earn $250,000 per year and cannot commit $500 to savings each year. These people spend everything they earn. This is very stupid, very foolish and very unhealthy. These families need to quit impressing their peers and neighbors and start getting excited about building their own net worth. There are some very happy families earning, saving and building net worth on $45,000 per year. They have fun and do not deprive themselves of a thing. Avoid the earn-and-spend way of life; it will kill your chances of building net worth.

You do not need to be a penny-pincher. You do, however, need to shop smart. Look for discounts. Buy household items and furniture only when on sale. Good, quality stores offer a number of sales throughout the year. Be a good sale finder. Look to the wholesale and big discount stores. Shop these stores wisely. They usually have items at a price less than you would pay retail. When food shopping, some people have made an art of laughing at the checkout clerk as they purchase $100 worth of groceries for $40 by using coupons for the big discounts. If you save coupons, you can sometimes buy groceries at 60% off the retail price. Look in your local paper for coupons or use the store app to see the discount offerings of the week. There is an old wives' tale that says you should go food shopping only after you have just eaten. This presumes you will shop healthier and wiser than if you haven't eaten since last night or you are shopping just before the feast.

Be selective in what you purchase. Be sure you will get good use out of the item purchased. It wastes money to buy some expensive item, use it once, then store it in the garage only to throw it away two years later. It wastes money to continually purchase state-of-the-art everything. Use the old appliance until it really does not work anymore. Your friends will admire your antique collection. Old products can work as well as new products. Buy new products selectively.

Cure yourself of the compulsive habit of buying all state-of-the-art electronics equipment. This equipment has functions and features most members of the household will never use or learn how to use. Beat the habit. Measure the utility of an item. Ask your spouse if you need it and if you will use it. Be certain you both agree on the usefulness of the item.

Impulsive shoppers are the targets of some advertisers. Don't surrender to these advertisements. Get in touch with your spending habits. Know whether or not you are an impulsive buyer. Work on reforming this habit if you have it. While you are doing this, always leave home without your wallet, money, credit cards and checkbook. It's a neat and free feeling to go out of the house without money or checks. Give it a try for a refreshing change. Do carry with you the necessary identification and driver's license, though. It's always a good idea to have a few dollars stashed in various places to be able to make a phone call in case of emergency.

Make a family spending policy that neither spouse will purchase anything without the consent of the other spouse if the purchase exceeds a certain dollar limit. Have your account require two signatures for amounts over a certain limit, if this will help make the policy work.

One of your duties in managing the family finances is to keep good records. Some of these records can be maintained on the computer. Most of these records are paper records you must file and store in a safe, damage-proof place.

Some of your transactions become part of your permanent records. Permanent records are those you keep for your lifetime, such as records of stocks, bonds or real estate you have owned; IRA accounts and notations of the year and amount of your IRA tax-deductible amount; and life insurance contracts and similar things that have important significance for future years. Part of your permanent financial records is a system of keeping the family's medical records.

Certain transactions are part of your annual records. Annual records are those such as your utility bills, auto registration and the routine expenses encountered each month and each year.

Each year you can throw away the annual records that are five years old. Most families keep their annual records in a box with the year written on the outside. These boxes are put in storage. Each time you put another complete year of records in storage, you can throw away the records from the oldest year. Thus you always have five years of records in storage to refer to for various reasons, including audits by the tax collector.

One of the key factors in saving tax monies is that you keep good records. This is a very important, if not the most important, tax principle this book can put forth. Keeping good records is even more important if you are self-employed.

Computerized records can help you keep track and compare where you are to where you should be. There are a number of easy-to-use software packages available in the marketplace for helping you keep good records.

You need to learn how to build net worth and preserve your wealth and relationship in the process.

You need to have a system of cash management. All companies in the United States have a system of cash management, and as good managers of your household, you need to have some good cash management techniques, too. You need to promise one another there will not be any month where there is negative cash flow. You need to eliminate deficit spending. Only the federal government has this luxury! Negative cash flow months are months that spending exceeds your net take-home pay.

You need to evaluate your present debt level. If you have any credit card or consumer debt, establish a plan to get rid of it by paying it off. Do not combine this debt into another mortgage on your home.

Using the worksheets provided earlier in this chapter, you need to establish a written spending plan for the year and each month. You need to review monthly your financial activity in relation to your monthly spending plan. Avoid becoming involved in a relationship with anyone who thinks that containing your monthly spending to something less than the amount of your net take-home pay is no fun.

Thoroughly discuss with your potential mate your plans for family cash management and the annual establishment of a spending plan. Do this before you decide to get married. Many marriages have gone on the rocks because this heart-to-heart discussion took place after the couple was married.

Work at increasing the percentage of your net take-home pay that goes toward making investments. While you are at it, don't forget to allocate some money for having fun.

At some point we need to look at the motives of the man and the motives of the woman who decide to get married. Are they planning to work together financially? Or is one so happy to get married and now they can begin spending the money and earnings of the other person? People over time will learn to have these discussions before marriage. This will leave the spend-o-holics to marry each other and then they can see if any of their theories will help them build a strong financial future!

Prepare a schedule or list of when you anticipate making capital expenditures for your household. If you plan to purchase a new car every four years, incorporate this into your monthly spending plan now. If you plan to purchase a family boat, set forth plans and start saving toward this goal. If you plan to replace household appliances, furniture, carpet, drapes or lighting, or if you plan to make repairs or alterations to the home, incorporate the year of acquiring or doing these items into your monthly spending plan. If you know your roof is going to need to be replaced ten years from now, make managerial plans to have the money available to cover this cost when the need arises. Build together some good financial management skills.

Plan to create a separate bank account that is used only for family emergencies. Some families have set out two accounts: one account with small monies for smaller, but agreed-upon, emergencies, and one account for big and unexpected emergencies. You will want separate accounts for the funds you use for additional family cash reserves. By structuring your accounts this way, you will have money available for emergencies should one occur. If you never have an emergency then you can stop funding the account once you have established a reasonable level of reserves to custom fit your family's situation.

A cash reserve should be established to cover loss of a job. This should be large enough to carry the family's monthly spending needs for a period of six months. This account should be bigger if you have a large home mortgage or a balloon payment coming due on your house.

Cash reserves are a puzzle piece you need in order to have a healthy and stress-reduced financial plan. With adequate reserves, you will not be forced to sell something you cherish, and you can avoid the bickering that could lead to the end of your marriage.

You will want to have an adequate amount of life insurance to protect your family in the event you meet with an untimely death. This is a must. I am not so keen on disability insurance, but all options should be looked at in this regard. It is amazing to me that people who have planned well and have become good net worth builders rarely end up with disability claims. They are usually so wound up and happy about their situation that they seem to not encounter needs for disability insurance. Work with your life insurance agent and custom fit your purchases to your family's needs.

You will need to plan early on, when your children are age two, for their college education, and you need to thoroughly discuss whether or not your children need a private school education. Part of joining the business world is the ability to get along with people from all walks of life. In public school, your child may learn the people skills necessary to become successful in the business world. I have seen a lot of money spent on private grammar school and high school education that seemed to have pleased the parents more than it helped the children join the world and become effective. Some religious schools in your community are categorized as private schools. They have helped some children become better students, and have helped them develop a sense of spirituality and responsibility that has become a very effective tool in the business world.

The decision to send your child to private primary or secondary school must be carefully evaluated. Sometimes you would be better off sending your child to the public schools. Put the private school tuition in a savings account in the child's name. Let that money grow and grow, then give them the money when they are 40 years old. You might be better serving the child's lifetime needs.

You should be careful to help your children and not burden them with lofty goals of your own design. Rather, encourage them to do their best at whatever they choose to do.

Some private school tuition can be tax deductible if you own your own business. Starting a family-owned business can be difficult, however.

You need to have an active discussion with your spouse about your plans to purchase or start a family-owned business. Family-owned businesses are known ways to build your net worth and shelter your income from taxation. The family-owned business is one of the last legal tax shelters available.

You need to make a commitment to find a family tax advisor who can provide you with the necessary information to minimize your annual income tax costs.

If you do not manage your tax situation carefully, over one-third of your lifetime earnings can go to the government by way of taxes. This same one-third of your career earnings could be put to work in your hometown, further building your own net worth. The secret to managing money and amassing wealth for a comfortable retirement lies in disciplined saving, wise investing, living within your means, and setting clear financial goals. Consistency, diversification, and financial education are key. Start early, prioritize retirement accounts, and seek professional advice when needed to secure your financial future, enabling yourself to retire in style.

You need to form specific plans of how you intend to "fund the gap." The gap is the financial difference between your Social Security and pension plan resources and the estimated costs of supporting your lifestyle upon retirement.

Funding the gap is the reason you want to build your financial resources. When you retire, you will receive a monthly payment from both your Social Security and your pension plan. From there, it is up to you to have created investment principal that spins off monthly returns to fill the gap between your monthly retirement income and your monthly retirement spending.

Here is a visualization exercise you can do now. Close your eyes and allow a few minutes to let your mind relax, then wander into your years of age 65 to 85. Go there and get a feel of what it will be like. Record in your mind where you will live, what your activities will be, what your health will be. What will be the source of your abundance? Where will your spending money come from? Stay in this space for as long as you can. Make a picture in your mind of all the details as to what it will be like.

Now on a sheet of paper jot down what your retirement years looked like to you with the visualization exercise. What were your activities? What was your health? What was your source of abundance? How much money will you need to meet your needs for the 20 years from age 65 to 85? What is your game plan?

MANTRA

I will be a wise and responsible financial manager with my daily actions.

CHAPTER 7

The Course We Travel Together

"Together we build with unity of purpose" should be the financial motto of your relationship.

Too many people get married without consciously being aware of exactly why they are marrying. They gain a certain feeling and act on that feeling. If you are open to discovering why you got married, please read on. You marry for some very specific psychological reasons. Most people do not structure the choice of a partner on financial considerations or have a range of partner choice that would be financially good for them. Some run off with the first person they fall in love with and rarely discuss finances in any meaningful way.

The modern romantic marriage can facilitate an individual's happiness and fulfillment, and it has the power for healing childhood hurts and wounds.

Earlier in the book we discussed that the impact, training and teaching your parents gave you helped you form your core belief structure. Many adults feel they were unfairly treated by their parents. Many adults feel that their emotional needs were not met by their parents. Many children are victims of emotional abuse by the parents. Some children were physically abused. Whatever your circumstance, your subconscious mind carries the scorecard of how you feel about the needs that were not met in your childhood. Thus, as psychological studies have shown, you have childhood wounds from your imperfect childhood. I found it necessary to learn more about this phenomenon to properly understand and guide married couples in successful financial management.

It is widely believed that marriage allows for full growth and healing of these childhood wounds. This principle has long been studied by people who watch and research human behavior. However strong you think you are in business, you still have these needs in your marriage relationship. You, too, have childhood wounds. These wounds need healing. The marriage relationship is the way to have these wounds healed and your needs met. You also need to recognize that your spouse has childhood wounds. These wounds also need to be healed, and your spouse's needs must be met.

In looking at your childhood and learning that your relationship with your spouse is the repair process, you begin to find yourself scrutinizing your childhood, identifying its malfunctions and shortcomings. The drive in your relationship is to restore your native sense of well-being and to feel and express the joyful feeling of being alive.

The experiences of your childhood have left specific wounds that must be healed in order to recapture your wholeness. That is the task of the relationship.

The task of your relationship is to heal your childhood wounds so you can recapture your feeling of wholeness.

With this feeling of joy and wholeness, you can then achieve happiness and commence enjoying your wealth together.

Read and reread these few paragraphs. If you begin to understand what is being said, you will be a much happier person in a much healthier relationship and save a fortune in professional counseling as an adult.

If you purchase books on relationships or attend courses or weekend sessions on relationships, you become more consciously aware of the many factors, issues and elements involved in a human married relationship. Most people enter marriage because they want to "be married" while giving little attention in how to "stay married" to the person you chose to be your lifetime partner.

Most people are driven to marriage due to the yearning for partnership, which is essential to the fulfillment of their vision. Without a partner, some people never feel whole. For both men and women, marriage serves as a profound union of hearts and souls, fostering love, companionship, and support. It offers a sanctuary where they can grow together, sharing life's joys and burdens. Marriage provides a sense of security, a partnership in navigating life's challenges. It's a commitment to stand by each other's side, through thick and thin, creating a family, and building a future together. Emotionally, it fulfills the deep human longing for connection, intimacy, and belonging, offering a unique bond that transcends the individual and creates a shared journey of love, trust, and shared dreams.

Most older singles seeking marriage partners do not relish the time they spend in the dating scene, although this is an essential and wonderful time for teenagers. Most married people do not relish returning to the singles scene. The idea that singles are free and independent, can travel anywhere and buy anything, then flag someone down, take them home and have loving wild sex is more myth than fact.

The dating process plays an important part in deciding to form a permanent relationship for the future. Both sides need to gain an understanding of one another. You need to discover your likes and dislikes and your commonalities, rate your compatibility and practice your communication skills. Find out if you are on the same path, can you cooperate with each other toward attaining a mutual goal. Are your goals mutual? Communication plays an important part in the dating process; both people should be open and honest and reveal themselves to the other. You should take time for intimate communication about every aspect of your life. You should discuss the past, the present and the future. You need to be open and available and have the ability to tell the other person what your true feelings are about the various things you have encountered in your life. You need to be able to tell the other person exactly what your needs, wants and expectations are from a more permanent and long-lasting relationship. This is the time to practice together your openness in communication. You need to be available and open while encouraging the other person to ask you questions about your past, for which you need to search down deep and provide open and honest answers. There are theories that women will be emotionally open in these discussions but men will struggle in discussing their emotions or true feelings.

From here, you make decisions about the future. You will want to discuss issues that are important to you. You each need to teach the other how to love you, in the way you want to be loved and touched. It would be unfair to say you liked x, y and z, then enter marriage, get comfortable and announce that really you like a, b and c. Most of all you have to start the process by evaluating your choice of partner. Is this a match in family background, beliefs, desires, economic achievement and spending habits? You need to have a frank talk about all aspects of financial matters. You need to frankly discuss what you would do in a situation where one partner works extra hard and accumulates while the other spouse produces a track record of financial waste. Do you believe it is fair to ask for half the assets and a bundle in monthly support from the person who marries you?

STRESS

Part of building net worth involves being able to manage stress. People who cannot manage their stress never become peak-performing individuals. Many parts of our daily lives cause us to have stress. We need to be able to vent and manage the stress we encounter in our lives.

Food, diet, relaxation and exercise are known to be helpful in managing stress. In order to be proficient in building net worth, you need to be healthy. You need to have frequent checkups and should employ the services of a qualified nutrition specialist. I have learned a lot about food from my friend Dale Figtree, a nutritionist in Santa Barbara, California. Dale designed a program using food and food combinations to recover from a bout with cancer. Since then, she has helped quite a few people understand how food and food groups help you with mental clarity, health and weight management.

A nutritionist can tell you what combinations of foods can help you build muscle, reduce fat and rejuvenate the vital organs. A healthy body and mind can accomplish a great deal in the arena of net worth building. It is surprising how many people of the younger set become health conscious once they have attained a level of financial success. Had they only been that health conscious in the early part of their career, they could have gone farther faster.

Do not manage your stress by eating or overeating. Regular exercise performed intensively should be used as a substitute for overeating.

Strong bodies support strong minds. Regular intense workouts refresh the blood, which in turn refreshes the mind and the entire body.

Many people like to demonstrate their wealth by going to expensive restaurants and ordering expensive, artery-clogging foods. This is why so many rich guys are fat. They want to show the world their wealth by dining at expensive restaurants and ordering complete meals of the most expensive items. They are either demonstrating their ability to buy the most expensive items or they are using food to manage their stress. Both are destructive and slow down the wealth building process. Look for these people, and you will find them. You'll know them because they are fat and huge.

Something dawned on me years ago that works so well you can save your money on all those diet centers. The only motivation a man needs is the insightful knowledge that women, including his mate, don't enjoy fat guys. They want to see those muscles and flat bellies. This should be enough to get the message to you to tune up your body.

COMPETITION

Healthy competition in the relationship can encourage higher earnings for both. Too much competition can be very detrimental, leading one partner to sabotage the other, to bring them down so the other can catch up.

Men are well known for their egos. You need to know that women have egos, too. Both of you need to have your ego stroked by your partner. You need to receive the proper recognition for your accomplishments. You need to watch that you do not try to compete with your spouse for higher earnings or speak too highly of your accomplishments to your spouse. Overdoing it will lead to resentment on the part of your spouse, and you will no longer be working compatibly in the same direction of higher achievement.

Celebrate achievement and thank your spouse openly for playing a vital part in your accomplishment. Learn to grow and work together in team play with unity of purpose. Support the ambitions and achievement of each other, it's a team! Do not openly compete with one another and build up resentment that will lead to problems within your relationship.

When an amateur athlete becomes financially wealthy through gaining endorsements and movie contracts, financial wealth pours into the household. You would think that everything is going to be great for that couple. All of a sudden you hear that the couple is getting a divorce. One of the problems in that relationship is that one spouse is doing fantastically well financially, while the other feels the need to compete but realizes they cannot attain that level. Somewhere along the line, possibly because a sport is an individual undertaking by one person, the couple was not working together to build. Now that one has achieved great financial success the other does not feel they played a part in that process. The couple cannot find happiness and celebrate together. Too wide of a gap has built up in the relationship and there is a strong feeling of the need to get out.

Competition amongst yourselves can be very detrimental to growth. Competition can be very detrimental to the financial building process. You need to grow and build together in your relationship. The liquid that flows between you, holding and bonding you together through all growth, adjustment and high achievement times, is the fluid mending and exchanging that comes with open and honest communication and communication intimacy with one another. Regardless of who achieves praise and support each other and be prepared to make some adjustments along the way.

Rather than open competition, both partners need to focus on wholly supporting the goals and ambitions of the other. Learning, knowing and helping each other attain their individual goals is much better than competing. Travel the road together. Share and celebrate in each other's joys, achievements and accomplishments. Always recognize and thank your spouse for the vital and important role they played in your accomplishment.

Remember to build all aspects of your life together with unity of purpose. There is an old slogan, "United we stand, divided we fall." This is a very true statement with respect to a long-term relationship. There are going to be high times and low times. There is going to be a time of high accomplishment and there may be times when you have not achieved what you set out to do. You need to be united at all times and share the ups and downs that everyday life has to offer. Being united allows you to share each other's growth.

Each year you are growing physically, mentally and emotionally. You will both grow at different rates and at different times. This sets forth the need for adjustments in your relationship. If you are communicating effectively, you will be united as you travel through these sometimes difficult adjustment periods together.

In order to learn and know the goals of your partner, you must engage in open and honest communication.

In setting your sights on building financial freedom, you need to know that there is a process of getting there. You do not all of a sudden wake up and find yourself wealthy. Usually, wealthy people accumulate money over time by converting their career earnings into meaningful investments that start generating return. You need to be united in your desire and search for investment profit.

The previous chapter discussed some of the basics of investing. Let's take a little deeper look into the reasons you need to make investments and the things to be watchful for. Let's get focused on a strategy for you and your spouse to jointly make investment plans for your family.

With unity of purpose let's take a deeper look into the investment world as you scan for opportunities that might be helpful to you and your spouse.

Investing requires some skill and knowledge. You will have to be an investment manager when you retire, whether you like the idea or not. You need to know and understand this now. When you retire, there is no one better suited to watch, monitor and manage your investable funds than you. Thus, you need to learn to watch and manage your funds at an early age. The sooner you become accustomed to becoming your own investment manager, the happier you will be and the more stable your investments will be.

You will need to manage your own account. You are best suited to watch your money. Once again, I remind you that professional investment managers and investment brokers are influenced by earning a commission each time you invest. If this is the case, they are tarnished and tainted about being objective in regard to your account. They might be more concerned about earning a commission than helping you have the highest yield on your investment. On the other hand, there are some perfectly fine, skilled and knowledgeable investment managers with a great track record of earning money for their clients.

No one understands your total financial picture better than you do. Often the broker knows you have $10,000 to invest. They do not know anything else about your financial assets. You know all about your financial picture. You know how available you are to take investment risk. Only you know your comfort level. You and your spouse know what your needs are. You and your spouse know exactly what your investment goals and objectives are. You and your spouse have the highest interest in protecting your family assets. You want your assets to be safe and secure while assuming a reasonable risk commensurate with the potential for investment return.

You need to develop your risk profile. This is a method of analyzing how much risk you can reasonably afford to take. This is determined by your age, your cash reserves and your overall asset holdings, your present net worth and your doctor's approval of the level of stress you should be exposed to. It is presumed that if you are young you can afford to take risks that are beyond normal levels. It is well known that if you are older you do not belong in risky investments. If you have developed massive amounts of net worth, you can possibly afford to take risks you would otherwise not take. No one likes to lose on an investment. You need to know your availability to take risks before you make an investment. This is done by analyzing your risk profile. A stockbroker or financial planner should be equipped to help you analyze your risk-taking ability and develop a present risk profile that is best suited to your needs.

You need to analyze your portfolio. Portfolio is a fancy word used in investment circles to refer to your entire investment holdings. You will want to do some statistical dissecting of your portfolio for diversification and investment management reasons. You should know what portion of your investments is in real estate and other kinds of investments. You will want to know what percentage of your stock is in what industry. You will want to know the percentage of your portfolio that is in cash and cash-equivalent investments, and what percentage of your stock investments is in income, growth and foreign stocks. Let your analytical self go free with your portfolio and develop management percentages that help you keep track of your affairs.

People who stay home each day and make stock trades from their living rooms take these same steps. They constantly do statistical analyses of their stock holdings to ensure they are diversified. They take into consideration foreign news and foreign affairs and the state of the economy, both domestically and globally. By watching and tuning their portfolios to these well-known indicators, they keep their portfolios better managed and more aligned to achieve profits.

You do not need to do hour upon hour of analysis and research the way a professional investor would. To know of their techniques is important. It is always helpful to do some homework with regard to your investments. You should be familiar with the economy, politics, and foreign and domestic affairs. Be on the lookout for companies or industry groups that will prosper in the days ahead based on what you see today in the well-known indicators. You may not be a professional, but you could certainly learn to be a good student of the investment world.

You and your spouse are going to be the investment managers for your family's assets. It is better to become comfortable with this idea at an early age. This is because the amount of your entitlement to Social Security, your IRA savings, your pension and the other contributing factors to your retirement nest egg most likely will not provide enough money to allow you to stop work and retire. You must make up that difference, "the gap," during your work career.

The more you can learn about investments, the better off you and your family will be.

You need to set aside a percentage of your annual earnings to fill the gap so you can permanently retire. Again, filling the gap refers to the additional amounts you will need as principal accumulations so you can permanently retire in style. Social Security payments are not going to be enough for you to live on.

Your retirement income will be made up of your Social Security benefits, the pension from your employer and contributions to your IRA account. Most likely, this will not be enough monthly income to support you. You need to recognize this at an early age and begin funding that gap. The gap is the mathematical difference between your monthly needs and the Social Security, employer pension and IRA amount. To summarize, your investment income minus your economic needs is the size of the gap that must be funded during your working life. Please understand this simple principle.

Some people are motivated to fund this gap. Some people are motivated and excited about financially accumulating. They work themselves into businesses and opportunities that create income and wealth far beyond their retirement needs. Try to identify the kind of person you are.

In dealing with your investment program, you need to focus on how to make your investments grow. You need to learn about and become consciously aware of what will make your investments produce income. You need to learn the cardinal rule of investing:

Whatever you invest in, you must preserve the principal portion of your investment.

You need to understand how and why you want to diversify your investments. You want to diversify (put your investments into a variety of investments or spread them around) to take advantage of ups and downs in the various industries and types of investments. This theory follows the good advice of not putting all of your eggs in one basket. Different investments allow you to be invested in different industries. By *diversifying* the eggs or putting them into different baskets, they will never all be broken at the same time. If you put all of your eggs in one basket, there is the chance that the eggs will all become broken.

By diversifying your investments, at any given time you will have some that do well and some that do not. The average performance will be acceptable to you overall. To understand diversification, look in the financial pages of the newspaper or in The Wall Street Journal. Look up the different mutual fund companies. See that each mutual fund company provides you with 10 to 60 different funds to invest in. Each fund is in a different industry or involved in a different strategy than any other fund in the family of funds. You can diversify by investing in a few mutual funds in one company's family of funds. Then you can skip over and invest with another mutual fund company. This is a way to diversify if you are investing in mutual funds.

Learning which mutual funds or ETF's to purchase requires doing some homework. You need to locate the financial pages of a newspaper. You could look in Investors Business Daily. This publication lists the top-performing mutual fund companies for this year, for the last five years and for the last ten years. You can see which companies and funds have performed well. Do the same with the ETF's. There is one certainty you will find in your research: The top-performing company one year isn't going to be the top-performing company the next year. Avoid jumping in too late. Do not invest in a fund only because it is the top-performing company one year. Investigate their long-term track record. Invest in those funds that have a long record of being listed among the top-performing companies.

Another tip about mutual fund and ETF's: You have to stay in for the long term. You cannot bail out with the slightest downturn of the market. Mutual funds will allow you to withdraw without penalty. Your funds are not locked up in the fund, but you should leave your investments in mutual funds in the market for ten years or longer to maximize your return on the investment. You will have some good years, you will have some bad yield years. On the average, you should do well by investing in mutual funds. Do not be impatient and pull your money out too soon. Hang in there. Invest for the long term. You will then enjoy the benefits. Be sure to invest in the direction of known up-coming trends and industry or technology break throughs.

Evaluate the effect of compounding. See how your invested funds will grow and grow.

If you invest initially $20,000 it may grow like this:

Years 1- 5	$20,000 goes to $40,000
Years 6-10	$40,000 goes to $80,000
Years 11-15	$80,000 goes to $160,000
Years 16-20	$160,000 goes to $320,000
Years 21-25	$320,000 goes to $640,000

Now in doing this you only invested $20,000 initially. If you add to this each year an amount of $200 per month ($2,400 per year), you would have over a million dollars just from your mutual fund strategy. Note that the monies you put into the investment are not large sums. You merely held in there for the long term and let the power of compounding work for you.

If you are investing in common stock, you will want to invest in common stock of reputable companies under a strategy that is suitable for you. You can diversify by being sure each common stock is involved in a completely different industry. Having investments in different industries allows you to have a diversified portfolio.

If you invested $10,000 in Amazon stock in 2003 in 2023 that one investment would be worth $780,000. If you invested 10,000 in Apple stock it would be worth $2,213,000 in 2023. You need to be able to see the trends.

Investments should be made with economics in mind and not because of some unbelievably wonderful tax result. The Tax Reform Act of 1986 put a stop to many investments that had tax motives as the leading thing that made the investment good. Investments driven by taxes may seem too good to be true, and they usually are. You will probably lose all of your money and end up with a tax audit to boot. You should make wise economic investments, and if they happen to have some sensible, favorable tax result, this might be the kind of investment you seek. Base your decisions on economic factors and the likelihood of your investment being returned to you with a sensible yield.

For your stock investments you need to consider a subscription to a stock advisory service or view a copy of one periodically in your local library. The Value Line Investment Survey is quite useful to the novice investor. Call and ask for the Money and Marriage discounted subscription price.

This firm provides stock analysis and information on a company-by-company basis that is segregated by industry. To properly diversify, remember that you want stock selections that come from different industries. This publication will give you an idea of the industries and the specific companies available. The survey includes a risk measuring system you might find useful, although it may appear to be complicated at first. The publication provides lots of information as to how to use the service and interpret the symbols and ratings it provides.

Another thing you will need to understand if you are going to invest over a period of years is the principle of "dollar cost averaging." Dollar cost averaging has to do with the fact that you might like a particular stock or mutual fund and you feel strongly about the future of that investment. Thus, you systematically invest a fixed sum on a monthly basis in that investment, regardless of the cost of the investment at the time you make the investment. Thus, you are investing a set sum of money, although the price of the stock may fluctuate up or down each month. Your strategy is that you do not care what the cost of the stock will be. You want the stock in your portfolio. The company whose stock you are buying is going to do well enough over the long haul. Thus, you accept the outcome of purchasing the stock at different high and low price levels. You plan to be happy with the return on your investment over the long term.

For the most part, you have to invest in your wealth building program, because if you bury the money in your backyard or sew it into the mattress, you will have no earnings on the principal. If you invest in low-interest savings accounts, you may have some earnings, but these earnings will not keep pace with inflation. If you put money in the bank, you want it to have more spending power in five years than it did when it was deposited.

There are many investment opportunities out there, and many of them are very bad investment opportunities. You, as the investment manager, must sort them out. You and your spouse are going to be the investment managers for your family's assets. It is better to become comfortable with this idea at an early age. Some examples of frontline investments available to the small investor are as follows:

U.S. Treasury notes, bills, bonds
Municipal bonds
Corporate bonds
Corporate stock
Mutual funds
Tax-free investments
Limited partnership offerings
Real estate
Your family-owned business
Bank savings accounts
Bank paper investments
Mortgage investments
Equipment leasing

College prepayment plans
Your own continuing education
Life insurance
Franchise business opportunities
Oil and gas (be extra careful)
Natural resources
Annuities
Movies
Artwork
Collector's items
Precious metals
Gems and coins
Foreign currencies

Real estate can be broken down into many components:

Apartments
Commercial buildings
Duplexes, triplexes, fourplexes
Historic rehabilitations
Industrial buildings
Low-income housing

Mini-storage facilities
Office buildings
Raw land developments
Shopping centers
Single-family residential properties

In making an investment, you need to know you will get your principal monies back. You need to know what the effective annual yield will be on your investment, and when all of your principal and all of your investment earnings will be returned to you. The older you are, the more you need to be concerned about having the investment earnings paid to you annually. The older you are, the less risk you are willing to take, for it may be hard for you to re-earn your principal if you lose it.

In addition to risk management, diversification and annual yield, you need to be concerned about the effects of inflation on your investment. Inflation is a factor to watch for in making investment decisions. Inflation is something that happens with the economy and the strength of the U.S. dollar. If inflation exists, you will not have the same spending power with one dollar in five years that you have today.

Here is an example of how inflation can eat up your savings. Today you may have enough money to buy a new refrigerator. If you were to put the money the refrigerator costs into your savings account today and let the interest build up, then in five years you would find that you do not have enough money in the account to purchase the same refrigerator. Inflation has occurred, and thus the price of the item has increased at a rate higher than your interest rate at the bank.

You may have earnings on the principal, but at the end of five years, because the inflation rate was greater than your interest rate, you will not have enough money in the bank to buy that same refrigerator. If your five-year average interest earnings are 3% and inflation is an average of 5%, over those five years your spending power has eroded or diminished.

This is an example of how inflation erodes your savings and will put you off course when you set your investment goals. Inflation serves as a threat to your financial security. Inflation eats away at the dollar, so the same dollar buys less each year.

A good hedge against inflation is to purchase rental real estate. If there is inflation you may adjust the rent to reflect these monetary changes in the marketplace. Thus, when you retire, you merely raise the rent to keep yourself in step with inflation. It's easier to raise the rent than it is for you to go to your banker and convince the bank to raise the interest rate it is paying on savings accounts.

Your portfolio is the whole book of investments you have within your investment holdings. When you talk about your portfolio, you are using one word to say this is what's happening to your investments as a whole.

In order to become a good investor, you need to understand that when you move money out of your bank account into other forms of investment, you are assuming some risk. Risk management is part of being a good investment manager. You and your spouse are going to be the investment managers for your family's assets. It is better to become comfortable with this idea at an early age. You want to take some risks, but you do not want to take huge risks or uninformed risks. Your risk can be minimized through education and knowledge. Take courses, read books. You can do this whether you went to college or not. Minimize your investment risk by educating yourself.

If you want to know how long it will take to double your money in an investment, you can use the well-known "rule of 72." This rule is a quick and approximate way to estimate the time it will take for an investment to grow significantly due to compound interest The rule is mathematical and goes like this: Divide 72 by the average rate of return (percentage earned per year) to calculate how many years it will take to double your investment. For example, if you have an investment that earns 10% return per year, divide the constant multiplier 72 by 10 (the percent rate of return). This equals 7.2 years for doubling an investment at 10% rate of return. A $10,000 investment earning 10% would then take 7.2 years to total $20,000.

You can work this formula in another way. If you know you have eight years to fund $40,000 for a college education, you can calculate the yield you will need or the initial investment you will need to make in order to achieve this financial goal. Divide the constant multiplier 72 by 8 (years), which equals 9. Thus 9% is the yield you will need to double an investment in an eight-year time period. You therefore need to invest $20,000 today at 9% per year to have $40,000 to spend on college education after eight years.

If an investment idea you are investigating seems too good to be true, it probably is. You want to carefully evaluate your investment idea before you invest. If all systems are go, then you take a calculated risk that you will not lose your principal sum. You are going to have to take some risks, because if you invest too conservatively, then you will not earn enough to keep up with inflation. You will not have enough money to retire on schedule.

Periodically you need to compute the yield on your investments and evaluate each particular investment's worthiness as part of your portfolio. Yield is calculated in a very easy way. Only simple math is involved.

You need to know about division—the numerator (top number) and the denominator (bottom number). The numerator is the amount you get each year as your earnings from the investment. The denominator is the amount you invested at the beginning of the year. For example, $500 annual earnings on a $2,000 beginning investment will equal 25% yield on your investment.

You need to personally calculate the yield on all of your investments at least annually. Do not rely on or read your yield from the bank, brokerage firm or investment house. To be a good investment manage do you own calculations to evaluate your investments.

Calculate your yield, then tell your bank, brokerage firm or investment house about it. This will let them know you know how to calculate yield, and that you are watching what they are doing with your money.

Next, you need to be able to calculate "total return," the total you made from your investment divided by the number of years it took you to earn the total return.

Let's say you put in $10,000 and got back in four years a total amount of $25,000.

$$\begin{array}{r} \$25{,}000 \text{ total return} \\ -\ \$10{,}000 \text{ beginning Investment} \\ \hline \$15{,}000 \text{ earnings on investment} \end{array}$$

Then:

$$\frac{\$15{,}000 \text{ earnings on investment}}{\$10{,}000 \text{ beginning investment}} = 1.5$$

This 1.5, when converted to percentage, is 150%. Then divide 150% by the four years it took to earn that amount on your investment:

$$\frac{150\%}{4 \text{ years}} = 37.5\%$$

Thus, 37.5% is the annualized return on your investment. This same calculation can be used if you only owned the investment for 42 months.

Although some math is involved, it is important to be able to do these calculations. This is part of your job as your own investment manager. You and your spouse are going to be the investment managers for your family's assets. It is better to become comfortable with this idea at an early age.

If you invest in real estate, the industry is full of rules of thumb that involve calculations like these. It is wise to become familiar with these rules and formulas and then do the projections and the math before you invest in real estate. There are rules of thumb that will help you calculate purchase price and amounts not to exceed in improvements in order to achieve a fair return on the time and labor invested. Square footage, unit cost information and formulas are very helpful when making a purchasing decision.

The more you learn about real estate, the more you discover there is a math formula to help you evaluate real estate.

Historically, real estate as an investment has done well during times of economic growth or inflation. Real estate profits are available when you thoroughly understand the economic principles of supply and demand. Real estate profits are available when you own the supply and the market is such that there is strong demand. Many fortunes have been lost in real estate by investors improperly reading or totally disregarding the laws of supply and demand and the leading economic indicators. Real estate is not very liquid and is therefore a long-term investment. It is quite cyclical in its pricing.

Real estate values tend to decline during times of recession. If you do not sell the real estate, you haven't lost anything. During bad times you should stay in the real estate market because you have sufficient cash reserves and can then reap your profit when the cycle moves upward.

Whichever direction you prefer, you should own at least some real estate and some common stocks. Your common stock holdings can be done through investment in ETF's or mutual funds. Whatever you invest in, make the investment of your pooled or community funds together with unity of purpose.

In today's economy, with your desire to retire comfortably, you cannot any longer afford to ignore investments and consider them only available to rich people. You, too, can accumulate and build wealth. You will need to build your wealth and then invest the principal sums of your accumulated wealth into solid investments that will pay a reasonable rate of return for the risk assumed.

Too many people work their jobs and spend all of their earnings along the way. When they retire, they have to sell their house to have investment monies available to provide for daily living expenses when they want to quit working. Why wait until you are 65 to discover you will have to develop some skills in investing your money? Why not develop these skills when you are 25 years old, then hone and practice these skills for 40 years until you are age 65?

You will need to break the cycle of earning and spending. You need to set aside some monies annually toward furthering your principal sums that are invested. Dedicating monies toward investments requires mutual decision, modification of spending habits, and team play to help each other increase the amount of investment earnings each year.

The "earn and spend" mode can be a double-edged sword when it comes to amassing wealth. While earning money is essential, how you spend it plays a crucial role. If you consistently overspend or indulge in unnecessary expenses, it can hinder wealth accumulation. To build wealth effectively, it's vital to balance earning with wise spending and saving. Creating a spending plan, investing wisely, and avoiding debt are key strategies. Ultimately, your financial success depends on your ability to manage both the earning and spending aspects of your financial life prudently.

MANTRA

Together we will build a strong financial future with unity of purpose.

CHAPTER 8

Planning Your Financial Health

Estate planning, tax planning and financial planning should all be concepts you actively discuss with your lawyer, your CPA, your insurance agent and, if need be, your qualified professional marriage counselor.

ESTATE PLANNING

Estate planning consists of the steps you take to pass the wealth you have accumulated to your heirs so governmental agencies do not break up your wealth creation. The gifting concept of wealth preservation is a very hard concept to learn after you have built up your financial net worth. It is the letting go that is difficult after building a solid business and other financial assets.

Your estate includes all of the things you own at the time you die, whether it is real property or personal property. This includes your house, your jewelry, your shoes and your toothbrush. Your estate is everything you own at the time of your death less the debts you owe to others.

There is a tax levied at death on the size of your estate. This is your estate tax. The value of your estate is determined by listing everything you own at its "fair market value" (FMV) at the time of your death. This would be the value you would receive if you sold everything and converted it all into cash before you died. The rate of estate tax is applied to the net fair market value of the assets you own at the date of your death. Thus the fair market value less the debt is the "net, fair market value." After applying your exemptions and credits, what remains is the taxable amount of your estate, referred to as your "taxable estate." The amount of tax can be staggering if you haven't planned in advance.

The current estate tax rates and your current exemption amount can be found on the IRS web site. For our discussion let's assume that the estate tax exemption amount is $600,000. If you have assets with a net-fair market value of $600,000 or less, you will not have an estate tax to pay at all. If your estate is larger than $600,000, then you begin to owe a tax. For example, if your estate has net assets over $1,500,001 but less than $2,000,000, you will owe an estate tax of 45% on the amount in excess of $1,500,000 plus the tax of $363,000 on the base of $1,500,000. On an estate of $1,800,000, you could owe a federal estate tax of $498,000. This means you heirs would write a check to the IRS for $498,000. Obviously, they would have to sell something to be able to do this. Please note that the estate tax rates and exemptions change at the whim of the Congress. In this book we lay out examples of rates and numbers so you can get the gist or idea of how punishing the estate tax can be for people that fail to properly plan their estate tax issues. At higher levels of estate value, you could owe a tax of more than 50% of your estate's net worth. This is not a very pleasant thought when you consider how long it took and how hard you worked to accumulate your assets.

The loopholes include giving all your assets to your spouse, thus no tax is owing. This can be done by the use of the unlimited marital deduction. The unlimited marital deduction for estate tax purposes says you can give your entire estate to your spouse and then you pay no estate tax at all. But when your spouse dies, then your assets will be gobbled up in estate taxes.

The old joke among estate planners is that when you die you give all your assets to your spouse. Then in a few years when your spouse marries someone 30 years younger than they are, they can pass all the assets to the new younger spouse and pay no estate tax. This can keep happening over and over again with no estate tax paid at all. Although this is great classroom humor, the idea does not leave anything for your children. Sounder planning ideas can be found.

Other loopholes involve the use of trusts and estate planning techniques, asset positioning techniques, and creation of life estates and charitable giving after your death so you do not pay an estate tax.

It is important to know the size of your estate so you can make lifetime plans not to have your wealth creations taxed at the time of your death. The way you hold title to certain assets can have meaning and impact at the time of dealing with your estate. There are differences between holding title to something as joint tenants, community property, sole owner or tenants in common. Ask your lawyer and tax specialist what these differences are and what different tax results they might have.

The significance of how you hold title is mostly an estate tax matter.

It is important you tell someone where they can locate all your documents, permanent records and the vital information about your financial affairs. You need to tell someone in exactly which drawer and in which county, state and country the drawer is located!

You need to tell this to both your spouse and the person who will be the executor of your estate in the event your spouse is not the executor. Inform this person, or better yet make an entertaining video for all the beneficiaries to watch. You can tell them what you think of them and what you leave to them and where they can find what you have left for them.

It is very difficult if someone is secretive. It is hard to find the assets to make a list of the estate. It can be hard to find the lawyer who drafted the last will. Plan to eliminate this burden for your family members in sorrow. Take someone into your confidence and tell them where they can find all of the key ingredients to your estate.

It is very difficult for family members to talk over with the parents or grandparents the issues of estate planning when those people are secretive. If this is the case, your best bet is to tell those in control that it would be wise to seek the professional help of an experienced estate planning attorney for the purpose of reducing the size of their taxable estate. Thus, the family wealth will not be reduced by the estate tax.

This can be a very sensitive family issue. The best you can do is to meet with a lawyer yourself to get advice on the proper direction to take. You may be endangering your lovability by giving relatives your ideas about their estate planning. This is often met with skepticism and the suspicion that you are trying to line your own pockets with their gold.

Some success has been met by having the family lawyer suggest a person see an experienced estate planning lawyer. The people with wealth have to become aware that nothing is forever; an annually published chart lists the average life expectancies in our society. Once they accept this inevitability, they may choose to not let the government benefit from their lack of planning or their poor planning efforts.

People with wealth may make proper use of trusts to give amounts of money to their loved ones. The trust document has directions as to who gets what and when. This can prevent those relatives who are not good money managers from getting a whole bunch of money at once. The trust can be set up to reward relatives who attend college and complete a college education. Monies can be given so that worthy business plans, when submitted by family members, can be funded. If you plan properly, a lot of creative things can be done sensibly so that the wealth, when created, is not taxed too heavily and also does not go to relatives who may lose or waste their inheritance. Wealth, when created, should be preserved for generations. You can start this process with wise estate planning steps taken early in the game.

LIFETIME GIFTS AS PART OF ESTATE PLANNING
Making lifetime gifts to other people or charitable organizations reduces the amount of estate tax you owe. Long ago many wealthy families learned they must make the necessary legal moves during their lifetimes to avoid the wealth-breaking estate tax. The Rockefellers are well known in estate planning circles for setting up their affairs in such a way as to minimize the impact of estate tax. These same legal moves are available to everyone for the asking when they hire an attorney who is familiar with the appropriate planning steps.

You can give to people or charitable organizations. Sometimes you can earn a present income tax advantage from making such gifts. You can gain current charitable deductions on your income tax return, avoid the capital gains tax on your income tax return or utilize the lower income tax bracket of younger family members. It is your obligation to yourself to find the top professionals who can plan and document these steps for you.

Gifting requires you to relinquish ownership and the control of your financial assets to someone you care to provide for and who is expected to live longer than you. You may give anyone up to $600,000 of the net assets from your estate and pay no estate tax. Each calendar year, you may additionally give $17,000 and your spouse may give $17,000 (annual total of $34,000 from the two of you) to any individual you choose. This $34,000 level of annual giving per recipient does not require you to pay a gift tax, file a gift tax return or reduce your lifetime gift and transfer allotment of $600,000. Thus, you can make transfers each year during your life so your estate will not have to pay a high estate tax. This way more of your estate goes to your loved ones or charitable organizations.

Each year you and your spouse together can give $34,000 to anyone in the world. If you have five children and they each are married, there are then ten people who would be very appreciative donees. Thus, you can give those ten people $34,000 each or transfer at the rate of $340,000 ($34,000 x 10) per year. Look what happens. After five years you have transferred $1,700,000 ($340,000 x 5) of your estate without using any of your lifetime exemption of $600,000. At this point, $2,300,000 would be exempt from the federal estate tax.

To accomplish this requires planning in advance and making annual gifts of your estate accumulations. There is a catch, too; any gift that is given within three years of your death may become part of your estate, due to a regathering or look-back clause in the law. This is to prevent you from making lifetime transfers within a few months or minutes of your death in order to escape estate taxes.

You can see how important it is to plan your estate so you do not get taxed by surprise. If you plan, it is easy to avoid paying estate taxes. Estate taxes are paid by families who fail to plan.

SUCCESSION PLANNING AS PART OF ESTATE PLANNING

If you own a family business, you should plan in advance for the succession of the enterprise. Are relatives going to run the business in the event of your death? Is this your plan? Is this their plan? Know that people cannot show up one day at the office, especially the day after your death, and pick up the pieces and start running your business. You need to properly plan for the next generation to graduate to full control and management of the business through years of training, grooming and hands-on experience.

The most important thing is that you make widely known and provide in your will or trust agreement for the way you see the business being run or sold after your death. It is very important that you leave a plan of how you think the business should be run after your departure. If you really want the business to stay in the family, you need to train the younger generation to run the company the way you want it run. The only way they can do this is to give up power and control of the company for periods of time so the new management can get the necessary hands-on experience of making real-life business decisions. They learn to be resourceful this way. They get some real experience as entrepreneurs. You get to come back on Monday morning and meet with them and provide training and guidance in how you would have handled the same situations.

You would not want to be on a plane headed for Paris from Chicago and find out the 40-year-old pilot had a heart attack and the second-in-command was just taking control of the airplane for the first time. This is a real scary thought. As a business consultant, I stress the need for succession planning and the release of control early enough for the second-in-command to get some hands-on flight time in all aspects of managing the business.

Family business transfer is very important to all involved. The parent is thrilled to see the business succeed. The child is thrilled to put forth effort and strive to do well. All of this needs to be protected by some well-laid plans. This is part of the job of the estate planning process.

Estate planning is the process of positioning your financial assets to minimize your estate tax costs while retaining enough income to retire in style. If you do not position your assets properly and in a timely fashion, your heirs will pay a lot of your hard-earned money in taxes. The estate tax was invented by government to break up wealth accumulations.

LIFE INSURANCE AS AN ESTATE PLANNING TOOL
Life insurance is an investment that provides liquid funds to your family in the event of your death. Life insurance can be used to pay down the mortgage on your home, provide income protection for your spouse and cash to pay any estate tax or inheritance tax that might be due.

If you plan to keep the business within the family when you have life insurance available to pay the estate tax, then the family is not required to sell your assets or the business in order to pay the estate tax when due.

Life insurance is a vital financial tool for individuals and families. It provides financial security by paying out a lump sum or regular income to beneficiaries upon the policyholder's death. This financial safety net is essential for covering funeral expenses, settling outstanding debts, paying off your mortgage and ensuring the well-being of loved ones. Moreover, life insurance can replace lost income, fund education, or support a comfortable retirement for dependents. It offers peace of mind, helping families navigate the financial challenges that arise when a primary breadwinner passes away, making it a necessity for protecting one's financial future and ensuring their loved ones' financial stability. When you meet with your life insurance agent also ask and lean the mechanics of a second to die policy. You can also inquire about other financial products like annuities.

Your agent is usually quite knowledgably and then they have people at headquarters of the company that can provide specialized knowledge.

The estate tax is real. It is due to the tax collector nine months after you die. It has to be paid in cash, not in business inventory or real estate. It has to be paid to a rather impatient tax collector in cash.

Life insurance is also a tool that will assist in the buy-sell agreement of a family-owned business. Whether you are going to sell the business to a family member or to your business partners, a source of cash to pay the family of the deceased person can be provided by life insurance.

As a tax planning measure for those of you who have life insurance, consider having a life insurance trust own the insurance as one of its investments. Be aware that if you do not do this, the life insurance you own will become part of your taxable estate. Depending on the size of your estate, the proceeds of the policy could be taxed at the rate as high as 50%, thus leaving only half of the proceeds from the policy for your loved ones.

If you do not want a trust, then an alternate method in doing your tax planning would have someone else be the owner of the life insurance policy that is paying off at the time of your death. Whoever is the legal owner of this policy will be the person paid, provided they are the named beneficiary and provided they have an insurable interest in you. This can be a spouse, son or daughter. The owner of this policy is required to make from their own funds all of the payments on the life insurance policy for the time it is in effect.

If you decide to set up a life insurance trust, there are many rules, advantages and disadvantages you will want to investigate before you proceed with purchasing the policy. Also, you need to set up the life insurance trust before you purchase the policy. This will keep the life insurance proceeds from becoming taxed as part of your estate. These monies in trust do not become part of the probate process. Most people have life insurance because it will help the surviving spouse get on their feet and be able to make payments such as the mortgage payment and the property taxes. Many times the non-working or lower earning spouse feels more financially secure when they know that there is some life insurance there in the event of some unexpected accident or sudden medical ailment occurs.

THE PROBATE PROCESS

In probate the lawyer representing your estate gets to keep a percentage of your entire estate. The fee is calculated on the total fair market value of your assets. It is not calculated on the net fair market value of your assets, however, but on the gross fair market value. Thus, if you have an estate with a fair market value of $1,500,000 and the estate has mortgages and debts of $1,000,000, your lawyer's percentage is not calculated on the net of $500,000. The percentage they apply to get their fee is against the gross of $1,500,000. They may tell you the probate fee will be 10% of the value of the estate, but they really mean 10% of the gross value of the estate. Thus, in this example, the fee is effectively 30% of the net fair market value of your estate. If you keep the money, valuable assets and property in a trust, the lawyer does not get a percentage of trust monies in calculating the statutory fee due to the lawyer through the probate process.

The probate process can be long and drawn out, and it will not allow you to have immediate access to the monies you have inherited. If your estate is less than $60,000, in most states you do not have to go through the probate process. If your estate is larger than $60,000, however, you must go through your states probate process to get title to the assets you have inherited. If you have a living trust, you will not have to take those assets through the probate process. This is the benefit of the revocable living trust because it helps you avoid the probate process altogether.

The trust document will designate who gets the money and when. You can protect your children from their creditors because the creditors cannot invade the trust to collect your children's debts. The trust assets are not part of your children's divorce proceedings should they become divorced. Thus, the trust saves taxes and is quite protective of the loved ones you care to provide for. To the extent you give money or property to your child from your trust then you can pass it to the child into their irrevocable trust. As you can see estate planning is complicated and complex. To achieve the best benefit, you have to align yourself with a working professional or professionals that specialize in estate planning.

LIVING TRUSTS, DO YOU NEED ONE?

One spouse may be pressuring the other spouse to create a will. One spouse-1 wants to give their entire estate to their two children from another marriage. This same spouse-1 after 6 months of marriage wants all the property of the other spouse-2 to be put half in their name. This requires changing the names on the deeds and the trust declaring each spouse owns half of each item of property. If spouse-2 dies unexpectedly then spouse-1 gets all of the proceeds from spouse-2 estate. These are the family knots that an estate planning lawyer sees many times.

Under this arrangement likely none of the money will go to the two children from another marriage of spouse-2. But spouse-1 may be satisfied with this arrangement because they just became the owner of half of all the property owned by spouse-2. They are 15 years younger than spouse-2 and will likely be the second to die. In this scenario either a referee needs to be called in as a consultant or therapist and then therapist and the attorney need to work together to see that there is a fair and square arrangement made so that the children of spouse-2 become taken care of in a reasonable way. Spouse-1 may be allowed to have some ownership in the property of spouse-2 but achieving half ownership may happen over a period of time and not after 6 months of marriage.

Many people are forming living trusts. When you go to the attorney's office today to ask for a will, the attorneys are explaining that the modern way of dealing with your affairs of your estate is through a revocable living trust.

If you have a living trust, you need to be certain that all of your assets have been transferred to the ownership of the trust. Many people forget to do this step. Thus, all documents that show ownership need to be changed at the time you form the trust. This is commonly forgotten. Many people have been in the attorney's office and told the attorney what assets the trust was to have. Those assets were listed in the trust papers that were drafted, but the documents evidencing ownership were never changed. If you have one heir who complains that you have not transferred the ownership of your assets to the trust, you run the risk of having those assets not covered by the trust go to the probate court. To probate court they will go, subject to the statutory attorney's fees and the months of a long wait for the probate process to end.

The revocable living trust helps save the long wait and costs of the probate process. If done correctly one minute after the deceased person is pronounced dead then the trustee of the trust takes over and has full control of all of the trust assets but must follow the direction of the trust agreement. So, one minute wait or a 24 month wait for the probate court to conclude, its your choice. You get to choose.

Once you choose the trust as the tool you want to use then you need to change the ownership documents and put the trust name on all bank accounts, automobiles, parcels of land, stocks, bonds and all other assets so the trust can become the owner of those assets. This step is called funding the trust. Many people forget to do this.

When husband and wife put their separate property into the trust, that property remains their separate property and does not by automation become community property. Everything can go into the trust and the separate property nature of the trust property is maintained.

If you purchase any property, real or personal, after the date you have set up the trust, be careful that you list the trust name as the owner of those items of property at the time of purchase.

The living trust is available to help you and your spouse save estate taxes. If you want to have the trust designed to maximize the use of your lifetime exemption of $600,000 of your estate's net fair market value, you may utilize one amount of $600,000 and your spouse may use another amount of $600,000. Thus, the family keeps $1,200,000 from becoming subject to the estate tax.

If you do not use a trust to provide for this, all your assets will pass tax-free to your spouse at the date of your death. Then when your spouse dies that estate will only be able to use one amount of $600,000 as the lifetime exemption from federal estate tax. Thus, the family would shelter only $600,000 of the net assets from tax when they could have sheltered $1,200,000 by using a living trust and describing this desire in the trust agreement.

In a living trust you and/or your spouse could become the trustee(s). You can appoint other people to become the trustee(s) when you die. You can appoint a bank trust department to become the trustee if you choose to.

Require the person recommending the living trust to submit in writing for your review all the reasons you should form a living trust. Then decide if the living trust is for you. The living trust is a valuable tool. From the main living trusts then, other sub-trusts can be set up at the time of your death to carry out all of your wishes over time so the beneficiaries do not get a big lump sum and then spend three years wasting and spending your money.

Your attorney should take some time with you and ask the questions of what you want to do with your estate, how do you see it being managed or disbursed over time. Many people set up a schedule of who gets what and for what purpose once the beneficiary has attained a certain age. Spreading the principal sums of your estate out over time will allow the beneficiary to more responsibly spend the proceeds of your estate. This is the most productive way to organize your estate and plan for the disbursement of the funds over time to set up the higher chance for responsible spending of the inherited money. There are many causes you can provide funds for such as education of the grandchildren, the starting of a business for a child, the purchase of a house. Most people appoint a trustee and through the trust documents tell the trustee to disburse annually the earnings on the principal sums held by the estate. Then upon attaining ages 30, 40 and 50 then a certain percentage of the estate principal is paid out to the beneficiary. Thus, estate planning if done right can be fun, exciting and done with the best interests of the beneficiaries in mind.

CHILDREN'S TRUSTS

If you have children and want to provide for them, you should consider using a trust to do so.

Children's trusts are something that can be regulated by the way they are designed. You design the trust, so you can specify the types of investments the trust can and cannot make.

You should not provide that upon your death your children get all your money. This is not prudent or wise. Either during your lifetime or by way of your will, create a trust that allows your children to receive the earnings from the principal sums you have left for them.

Allow them to draw down on the principal to attend college or for extreme medical emergencies not covered by insurance. Then distribute the principal to them upon reaching certain ages, such as 25% of principal distributed upon reaching the age of 30, 25% upon reaching 35, 25% upon reaching 40 and 25% upon reaching the age of 45, or some variation of this. The money will be spent more wisely and will more likely be kept out of creditor or divorce cross fire should problems happen with one of your children.

Additionally, your will and your trust can provide for those who wish to attend college or graduate school. You can set the criteria, standards and conditions so monies from your estate will be allocated for these purposes. You can also provide funds for your loved ones' well-thought-out "business plans" as a way for them to inherit some of your estate. Upon presentation of an acceptable business plan to a trustee, your trust can provide startup or working capital for the business. Also, if you have daughters, it is very important that you have provided your financial support for their wedding plans. The wedding day will be the most important day in your daughter's life. Be sure your estate planning has provided for this event. We see wedding plans often overlooked by estates of younger people who have died unexpectedly.

In summary: A revocable living trust is a crucial tool in estate planning, providing numerous benefits. It enables individuals to retain control over their assets during their lifetime while designating a successor trustee to manage them if they become incapacitated. Upon their passing, assets within the trust avoid the time-consuming and expensive probate process, ensuring a smoother and more private transfer to beneficiaries. This instrument also offers flexibility, allowing for amendments or revocation if circumstances change. It safeguards against potential challenges to the estate plan and may provide tax advantages. A revocable living trust streamlines asset distribution, protects privacy, and enhances control in estate planning.

THE LIVING WILL:
WHO AND WHEN TO PULL THE PLUG

A living will, also known as an *Advanced Healthcare Directive*, serves a vital purpose by allowing individuals to specify their medical treatment preferences in case they become incapacitated and unable to communicate their wishes. It provides guidance to healthcare providers and family members regarding end-of-life decisions, resuscitation, life sustaining treatments and organ donation. This legal document ensure that a person values and choices are respected, reducing potential family conflicts and helping medical professionals make informed decisions, ultimately promoting autonomy and dignity in healthcare decision making.

The *living will* declares that if you become terminally ill you do not want any extraordinary measures taken to prolong your life. A living will gives guidance to your family members and to the doctors providing you treatment. You can direct them not to use advanced measures to prolong your life if there is no reasonable expectation you will recover.

The living will is a way for you to specify if you want to be kept alive by use of mechanical devices. Note that the courts do not always grant your wishes. You also can specify if you wish to donate organs to others upon your death. The living will allows you to appoint someone you trust to guide medical efforts to keep you alive if something were to happen. This document will specify the type and duration of efforts that should be used in the event you are fatally injured. You can attach these plans to your normal will or trust document, or draft a separate document. If you want to provide instructions about your right to die to the family, doctors and courts, you should use strong language if you really do not want to linger after something serious happens.

CONGRUENT AND PARALLEL PLANNING

Financial planning needs to be integrated into your estate planning process. You need to align your financial goals with your other life plans. I cannot tell you how many couples have come into my office and told me something similar to this example.

A couple wants to sell their business so they can plan to start another type of business, more suited to their interests, in another part of the United States. Three weeks later they rush into the office to say they are interested in buying a new house in the community where their current business is located. This is a classic example of incongruent plans.

The big plan is to sell the business and move to another part of the United States. The time frame for doing this would be from six to twelve months. Why would they want to buy a home in this community? If they sold the home in month twelve, the selling expenses would eat up any profit they may have earned from purchasing the house. This illustrates the need for planning. The big plan should agree with the smaller plans. All plans should be running in parallel lines, not in lines that will ultimately collide with each other.

Daily I spot life plans that are not congruent with the over-all plan of the family. Thus you need to align your financial goals with:

1. Marriage goals

2. Child-rearing goals

3. Income tax goals

4. Asset acquisition goals

5. College tuition strategies

6. Retirement plans

7. Estate planning strategies

Your plans need to be properly aligned so they are running parallel to each other. You also need to align yourself so your attitudes, mental outlook, emotional state and physical self are all aligned to meet your goals for abundance and increased financial net worth. Remove those barriers that are preventing you from obtaining greater wealth.

CYCLICAL BUSINESSES

Some households have both spouses in industries that produce salary, bonus, commission or other types of income that fluctuate widely—very high upswings and very low downswings. Thus the household income can also swing violently upward and downward year to year.

This is best illustrated by looking into a household where one spouse is a building contractor and the other spouse is a Realtor. When times are good, there can be a lot of construction activity and a lot of homes sold. Thus this household can have a few years of high income. Then through no fault of their own, the market and the economy shift. They then have three years of very little income. This can cause problems.

The next example is not a household where violent swings occur. The types of income coming to the household complement one another. Complementary income would exist where one spouse is in the construction industry, primarily a summer income activity, and the other spouse is a winter ski instructor, thus providing the household with summer and winter income. This is an example of complementary income.

In the example of the contractor and the Realtor, when the building industry is doing well the household has high income. When the economy and the market turn downward, both incomes dry up and go away, leaving the household with no income until the economy turns upward again.

Worse yet, consider the household where one spouse is a building contractor and the other spouse is a homemaker. The homemaker has grown accustomed to spending freely and often during good times. The homemaker has grown accustomed to not working outside of the home. For the contractor, business has been good and is getting better. Once financial times get good, everyone wants to forget the lean years and they want to bask in the sunshine of the good years. The last thing people want to do is return to financially lean times after times have been financially good.

Look what happens to the contractor and homemaker household when all of a sudden, the market and the economy shift. Business tapers off. The contractor starts letting out a few whimpers at home that business is not good. It is very hard to come home and say, "Dear, business is terrible and getting worse. Secure the house for the financial storm ahead." When the contractor tells the homemaker that business is not good, the homemaker seems to say, "Thanks for telling me dear, I hope business gets better."

This explains the need for communication intimacy—frank, open, honest communication with pencil, paper and pictures. Otherwise, this is going to become another construction household ending with divorce. The contractor does not clearly and effectively communicate that business is going from bad to worse. At the same time, the homemaker has grown accustomed to the luxuries of life and spending habits of financial good times and does not want to hear that business is going badly and is expected to get worse. That would cause cutbacks in lifestyle and spending. Herein lies a huge problem. Normally, in this same household, you have two people who love each other. These people would walk a hundred miles barefoot in the snow together to build a strong financial future. They are often a very united couple in many, many ways.

Because one does not want to announce and the other does not want to hear or accept that they will be having financial reversals and that lifestyle and spending must be cut back drastically and promptly, communications begin to break down. Neither spouse is supporting the other. Complications set in. One spouse begins to resent the other. They begin to ignore each other. One of them might then drift into the arms of someone else. Relationship deterioration sets in. Soon things go from bad to worse; trust, confidence and understanding break down. Divorce or separation is just around the corner.

This could all be avoided if the couple had good communication skills. These people first need to know that the business of the family is a cyclical business. The upturns are great and the downswings are terrible, but united they stand. These people need to know that the construction business is a high-risk industry. It is an industry subject to market conditions, to turns of the economy and to financial reversals if jobs are not bid correctly. If you bid incorrectly the construction business can go bad even in good times. When times are good, spouses always have to remember that around the corner times may get bad. You need to assure each other daily or at least often that you are in this life together: "Good economy or bad economy, I love you, and I stand by you. Please tell me if we are having good times or bad times right now!"

This kind of togetherness and understanding on the part of both parties is very important in stopping the current high divorce rate. Couples who are good at communicating with one another and ever ready for challenges and adjustments together will survive in their relationships. Those who do not plan to communicate, support and understand the other person in the relationship are increasing the chances of the relationship breaking apart.

It is not only construction households that are hit with the rise and fall of family economics. Upswings and downswings hit households that rely on many other industries. These upswings and downswings happen to self-employed people and those who are employed by someone else.

When financial times are good, it is easy to be united and together even though your communication skills may not be practiced. When times change and you are not communicating and adjusting well at the same time, problems will set in.

There are not many industries, or jobs for that matter, that guarantee each year will be bigger and better. I have seen these drastic financial reversals hit attorney households, medical households, farming households, sales households and highly paid corporate executive households.

Upward and downward swings to the household finances are real. If you are not properly informing each other and planning and saving for the downturns, then you are setting your relationship up for the disaster that will soon follow, sometimes with the first turn in the road.

Know that rather than plan, save and communicate, some couples have jeopardized their relationship and have been ill-equipped to handle reversals and financial bad times. As a consequence, these couples have divorced during downward shifts in their jobs.

Mostly this is due to the seemingly oblivious reaction of the home-maker. The homemaker does not equate a downturn of business to cutting back on spending and lifestyle. There must be a downward and drastic change in economic lifestyle to survive the market conditions if this relationship is going to survive. Many construction families set aside money for the shifts in the market. Those that do not are in for big trouble.

Ideally, if you are in a cyclical business the other spouse is in a business opposite to your cycle or in a stable employment wherein the income is steady regardless of market shifts in the other spouse's industry.

We have seen what cyclical businesses can do to a relationship. Together, you need to know what is happening with your household income. You need to rise and celebrate together and be ready for shifts, adjustments and downward turns together in order to survive.

FINANCIAL PLANNING AS A SYSTEM

In Chapter 6 we discussed the matters to consider in managing the household finances. This part of Chapter 8 is the advanced course in financial planning. Once you have discovered the need to keep good records, categorize and track household outflows and focus on investment rather than spending, you will want some additional information.

These more advanced financial planning steps are for those readers who are presently more advanced and those who have implemented the important steps discussed in Chapter 6.

Financial planning is a system of taking into consideration the whole of your financial assets and establishing a flexible plan to position those assets and help you reach, in a faster way, the specific financial goals and objectives you have established for your household.

There are many experienced financial planners in the marketplace. To find the great ones takes some searching and willingness to possibly travel outside your geographic area. The services of a financial planner are tax deductible in accordance with the provisions of Sections 162 and 212 of the Internal Revenue Code.

INCOME TAX PLANNING

This book does not dwell on the tax planning steps that you must take to minimize annual income tax costs. This is an important step. Your financial planning steps must be carefully integrated into your tax planning steps. Prudent business would indicate that your financial planning steps come first and then you take those steps necessary to save income tax costs. The tax laws are complex and require you to seek the advice of a tax specialist. You should not spend time with anyone who is not a CPA with a masters degree in taxation. You will pay the same fee to someone who is not, and why would you do that? There are plenty of good CPAs out there who have thought enough about their professional pursuits that they have invested their time and their money in advanced tax education. Your tax advisor should be one of these people.

Should you have an encounter with the Internal Revenue Service, it is always wise to have your tax professional represent you and handle the matter. You should stay at home and help your professional with your pleasant encouragement during what usually is a rather unpleasant experience.

Some unique tax war stories come to mind, one of which concerns an encounter with an appeals officer for the Internal Revenue Service in California. I asked the auditor to look at the common sense need for my client to have incurred these education costs and allow them as a deduction. The appeals officer's cheeks reddened as he picked up a copy of the Internal Revenue Code from the conference table. He held the book over his head and then slammed it down on the table. The book bounced at impact while the appeals officer shouted, "There is no provision in the Internal Revenue Code for common sense!" This statement broadened my understanding of the tax law. To this day it still holds true.

Tax planning is important. You can save a large amount of money with careful planning. The best way to shelter your income from taxation is to own a business that is run by your family.

CASH MANAGEMENT

Another important part of financial planning is cash management. This is the way you manage the cash that comes into your household. There is a concept in finance and net worth building called leverage. Leverage is the art of spending one dollar in a way that turns it into a higher multiple of dollars. Through artful cash management techniques, you can become the master of stretching one dollar into five dollars. You want to handle your cash so you do not pay your bills until they are due. If someone offers you a discount to pay sooner, take the discount and pay sooner if the discount is large enough to excite you to do so. You want to store your cash in an interest-bearing account until the last possible moment before making payment to your creditor.

The more common definitions of leverage consist of the ability to finance an investment with a small amount of one's own funds, such as a down payment with the balance consisting of borrowed funds. Leverage is the use of a smaller investment to generate a larger rate of return through borrowing. Leverage is the amount of money borrowed by a business person in excess of money or assets invested personally in the business. Leverage refers to the advantages that may accrue to your business through the use of debt obtained from third parties such as banks, lenders, investors or other outside people instead of investing your own funds in the business. Real estate studies tell you about OPM, "Other People's Money," as a means of purchasing real estate for yourself.

Leverage is used in real estate and other investments to gain a lot of return with very little of your money invested. With real estate, you might purchase a $100,000 duplex by paying $15,000 as the down payment. You use the bank's money (and the seller's money if they carry the loan) to make up the rest of the purchase ($85,000). Then you use the tenant's money to pay back on the $85,000 of loans you have. After four years, if there is positive cash flow in the property, you may still only have $15,000 of your money invested in the property.

In year four you sell the property for $135,000. You then will experience a leveraged return on your initial investment of $35,000. The $15,000 you put to work initially made you a financial return of $35,000 ($135,000 minus $100,000 = $35,000). This was earned in four years. That would be a 133% return your investment. This is calculated by subtracting your initial investment from your total return ($35,000 less $15,000 initial investment = $20,000 profit) and dividing it by the amount of your initial investment ($20,000 / $15,000 = 133%). Divide 133% by 4 years and you get a 33% yearly return on your investment.

You need to study this principle of leverage, since sensible leverage can help you earn a profit in the many endeavors you undertake.

Some people have mastered the art of using leverage and have understood another way to use the principle of leverage by remitting to their creditors in a way that maximizes the time they hold onto funds, earn interest on those funds, and then pay utilizing the bank's float.

When you write a check, your bank does not subtract from your account at the moment you write the check. The check is subtracted from your funds at the bank when the check is presented to your bank for payment by the vendor you gave the check to or by the vendor's bank. The delay time from the moment you write the check until the moment the money is subtracted from your account by your bank is called *float*. I have seen people with money market accounts pay their West Coast creditors with a check drawn from an East Coast financial institution, then they pay their East Coast creditors with a check drawn from a West Coast financial institution. In doing so they have added to the days of float. They have received credit for paying the bill and at the same time they have earned interest for a few extra days on the same money.

MORE ADVANCED FINANCIAL PLANNING IDEAS

Require your bank to make automatic withdrawals monthly and transfer them into your long-term savings account. This is a good way to continue feeding your investment program, and it is a service your bank will gladly provide. The transfer is made automatically by the bank's computer on a monthly basis in the amount you designate.

Advise your mutual fund company to automatically withdraw from your money market fund a stated amount each month. Have those funds directed into a particular mutual fund in that company's family of funds that shows high prospect for the future. Have your funds buy mutual fund shares each and every month without fail. Allow your account to grow and grow and grow.

Pay back thirty-year home loans and five-year car loans at a rate faster than required by the minimum payment each month. Make a monthly principal reduction payment by paying more than the minimum monthly payment. This will save you from wasting money that is only going to pay the interest on the early years of the loan. You are then applying more toward the unpaid principal amount of the loan.

Know the cost per unit when you shop in the supermarket. Some items are cheaper at one grocery store than at another. Know what items to buy at which store. Most grocery stores specialize in lowering the price of certain products so they can make claims of having lower prices than the other grocery chains. Know the unit costs per store. Know in which store to purchase which products. Know in which store to spend your coupons. Do not accept double savings when another store redeems for triple savings. Use those coupons. They are valuable and can cut your grocery bill in half. Compare products on a cost-per-ounce or cost-per-pound basis. Be careful that you don't purchase the big size only to find out that some of the product spoiled, became stale or the bugs got it before you did. The large size is not always the best buy per pound.

Purchase and mix natural ingredients. This may be less expensive and healthier. These foods will not have all the preservatives that ready-made foods do. Read the labels on the packages of the food products you are buying in the grocery store. You are paying a huge premium to have baking powder added to flour when you buy pancake mix, basil and oil mixed when you buy pesto sauce and oil and vinegar mixed when you buy salad dressing. Mix these things together yourself.

If you are a woman, you should try to go to a car repair facility accompanied by a man. Otherwise, look for woman-owned car repair facilities.

Many women's clothes, other products, and girls' products are less expensive if you purchase them in the men's department. Compare hair spray, cosmetic supplies and deodorant.

Watch what you spend in restaurants. Make your own flavored coffee. Do not buy something for $1.25 you can make for ten cents.

Maintain a list of names and addresses of all credit card companies. Make a note of the telephone number to call and the procedure to follow in the event you lose your credit cards or wallet. Some people just go to the nearest copy center. They empty their wallet onto the copier and make photocopies of everything in their wallet. This makes it easy to recover your important things if your wallet becomes lost or stolen.

Maintain a special metal box for the major items you purchase. Keep the warranty information, users guides and manuals for these major purchases in the box. You will have instant knowledge of where to find purchase documents and instructions as to how to fix or repair an item.

Teach your children money management skills.

Paying extra money as a principal reduction payment on your home mortgage is a good cash management step.

Planning in advance instead of walking into a financial rut is the best way to professionally manage household finances. There are too many people out there who have lost their jobs, then say, "Oops! We're out of money, honey!" If you are employed by a company, evaluate the national statistics about the chances of having a change in employment. You should have ready cash reserves to deal with this career challenge that likely will strike your household someday. If you are presently feuding with your boss or the upper management of your company, know your chance for layoff is greater than if everything is going very smoothly. I am always amazed at employees who have no savings, then lose their employment and put their real property in jeopardy. Simple planning in advance would prevent this. It is always wise to have on hand at least six months of net take-home pay in a semiliquid account to carry you through unforeseen difficulties.

Equally baffling is the college-educated couple who has required their children to study hard to get good grades so they will be admitted to college. These same authoritarians have done nothing to save for or fund their children's college education. They wander into my office in June of the year their child is to start school and wonder what can be done to meet the costs of college education. Planning in advance by professional managers would have started a college savings and invest-ment fund when the child was two years old. It is necessary to plan in advance. You need to make corporate boardroom decisions for your household the way good corporate managers plan in advance. Make them in the comfort of your own living room, with the help and cooper-ation of your spouse.

Another aspect of financial planning for fast-track participants is to inundate yourself with self-help books and tapes. The more you work on yourself in terms of setting and achieving goals, overcoming compulsive habits and working toward having a healthy outlook on life, the more you put yourself miles ahead of others who try to build net worth. In reading books and listening to tapes, you are helping to bathe and cleanse your subconscious in order to have positive inputs to help you get on the right track and become a winner in life. Instead of salivating and creating a list of things you want to buy when you have $1,000 sitting idle in a savings account. Learn to salivate when you can find an extra $100 to put into your savings account. Sometimes a change in thinking, a change in focus is good for your overall financial health. Avoid the best you can the unhealthy mode of earn and spend faster than you earn!

Continuing professional education in real estate and investments can help you. Education has been identified as the shortcut to experience. You can study how and when to invest. Get to know the behind-the-scenes secrets the pros know. The more technical knowledge you have, the more sure you are to limit your risk when making investments and dealing with real property for profit.

To explain how important goal-setting is, I will simply say goal-setting is the most important step to your success in building net worth. You need to have a clear, focused vision of where you are going in the future. You need to have goals. You need to have written goals. You need to check these written goals to determine if you are in a position to meet your goals. Make sure your goals are specific. Make sure your goals are written. Tell your spouse about your personal goals and listen to what your spouse's goals are. Decide together what your specific family goals are to be. Celebrate when any goal has been met.

You need to have an account for emergency cash reserves for a number of reasons. You need to increase the cash reserves you have as the amount of debt you encounter increases. Debt is your friend if you are using debt to purchase real property. Debt used to purchase consumer goods is your enemy. You want to avoid debt for purchasing consumer goods. The larger your monthly payments become, the larger your cash reserves should be. This holds true, too, if you own your own business.

Many people are forced out of business because they have too little in cash reserves. When business turns down for a medium period, without sufficient cash reserves you will not be able to make it through the slow period. Out of business you go. I have seen this happen to many good businesses. Many of them have closed their doors while the owners run around trying to sell off all their toys, including the airplane. It is really a shame to see a good business go out due to the overextension of the company by management. Sometimes people in business gain the feeling they have discovered the way to make a profit with the business. Then they go out and purchase second homes, boats and airplanes, only to learn the hard way that the increase in business was only temporary and now the downturn is starting. When the downturn hits, they do not have sufficient cash reserves to carry them through, let alone maintain the new and inflated lifestyle they have created.

Plan to have for your business and your family sufficient cash reserves to carry you through the unexpected.

WHEN DEBT IS YOUR FRIEND

In knowing that debt is your friend if you are using debt to purchase real property, you will want to have sufficient cash reserves to service that debt. You will want to plan for vacancies and the other unexpected things that could come up when owning real property. You will want to be aware of and avoid when possible, the date that balloon payments are to become due. Many Americans lost the real estate they once owned when they purchased property with the expectation of refinancing the property soon after the purchase date, only to find out that either the investor or the property could not qualify for a new loan. This leaves you in a very hot spot, usually with no way out. Avoid balloon payments if possible. If you have balloon payments, know and plan for the retirement of that loan on time so you do not end up losing your property.

If you are familiar with real estate and are seasoned due to many years of ownership of real property, then investigate; foreclosure sales for ways to purchase property at a deep discount. Foreclosure sales provide opportunity to the real estate investor who researches thoroughly. In bad times, many quality properties are auctioned on the courthouse steps. If you know the market value of property in your area, you should purchase these properties only when you are convinced your purchase price is at a deep discount. There are many difficulties and legal problems in dealing with foreclosure properties, and this avenue of acquisition is not for the novice or intermediate real estate investor. Your county will sell properties where the property tax was not made by the owner, these tax sales present opportunities for knowledgeable investors. Bankruptcy courts sell properties and the IRS sells properties in their own auctions. Become aware of all of these opportunities and more that exist in the marketplace.

The factor that keeps most people away from foreclosure properties is that usually you have to purchase the property with all cash. This is true, but there are many ways to work around this requirement. The simplest way is for you to establish a good working relationship with your banker. Bankers can extend lines of credit to you for foreclosure acquisitions. They will do so once they are convinced you know what you are doing when buying foreclosure properties.

You may also want to invest in second trust deeds or second mortgages (the terminology and procedure is different from state to state) on real property. The second mortgage investment is a way to invest in real estate without all the day-to-day problems with direct ownership of real estate. Your investment is secured by the real estate itself. If the owner of the property does not pay you, then you can capture the property in foreclosure and potentially pocket a profit larger than your initial investment. Second mortgage investments pay you an agreed-upon rate of interest that is usually larger than the bank will pay you on savings accounts. For example, if you invest $40,000 at 12% in a second mortgage, the owner of the property must pay you back in accordance with the terms of your promissory note, in this case, the $40,000 initial investment plus interest at the rate of 12% on the unpaid balance of the $40,000, usually received in monthly payments of principal and interest.

The most important rule in second mortgage investing is that you hire your own licensed real estate appraiser to provide directly to you an appraisal report on the property. If you make the investment, you can ask the owner of the property to reimburse you for the cost of the appraisal. You want to examine the existing loans on the property and compare all loans, including yours when in place, to the appraised value of the property. If the mathematical relationship of loan (numerator) and appraised value (denominator), when divided, is larger than 65%, do not make a second mortgage loan on that property.

The hazard with second mortgages is that if the owner of the property defaults (cannot pay you), likely they cannot pay the first mortgage either. If the first mortgage holder forecloses on the property first, you lose all of your investment in the junior loan, the second mortgage. To fix things so you can get your initial investment back, you must have enough cash and energy to pay the first mortgage holder all of the arrearage and continue to pay the first mortgage holder monthly, all while getting the property clear of occupants, fixing it up and selling it. If the owner defaults, then the second mortgage holder gets an immediate education on why second mortgage investments are so risky.

Many investors have done well with second mortgage investing, however. If you successfully foreclose on the property, fix it up and then sell it, you may get back much more than your initial investment. Say, for instance, your $40,000 second mortgage investment was provided to an owner of a property valued at $300,000 who had a first mortgage of $100,000. If the owner defaults, you foreclose and then sell the property. You stand to receive $300,000 less the $100,000 first mortgage, less your $40,000 investment. If selling costs were around $20,000, you could end up with $140,000 extra. If this happened within a two-year period, you would have earned 175% annual return on your initial investment ($140,000 / $40,000 = 3.5, or 350%; 350% / 2 years = 175%.)

The next step to take when you have become comfortable with second mortgages is to consider purchasing existing promissory notes for cash on properties that already have the second mortgage in place. This opportunity occurs when the seller is forced to take back a promissory note when they provide seller financing. Sometimes these sellers want to convert the promissory note into immediate cash. In this case they are willing to sell the promissory note, secured by the real property, for less than the face value of the promissory note. For example, if a seller is required to carry a $40,000 second mortgage, that seller may be willing to sell that promissory note to an investor for $30,000 in cash. If, as an outside party to the transaction, you purchase the note, you help the seller by giving them cash now. It helps you because you have a long-term investment, secured by real property, where you will be paid by the owner of the property the full $40,000 plus the amount of interest stated in the note. Your return on investment may be 12% by way of your interest collections and 30% by way of the fact you paid $30,000 and got $40,000. This is an additional $10,000 return on the investment.

Let's review the second mortgage you purchased for less than face value. You invested $30,000 to get $40,000 plus interest at 12% on the unpaid balance of $40,000. If you held this investment for five years, your effective average annual return on the whole investment would be approximately 22%, all secured by real property.

These types of investments in real estate are complex. Before you attempt a transaction of this kind, you need to be supported by the appropriate professionals, especially your attorney, your appraiser and your Realtor. With this team, you will learn of the ramifications of the transaction and the risks involved, and you will have a fair estimate of the value of the property before you invest your funds. Once you master this form of investment, you can make a fair return on your invested funds. Often you will see in the classified sections of newspapers that people are offering to buy second mortgages. These are private investors who are willing to buy for cash second mortgages at a price that is less than the face amount of the unpaid balance of the mortgage.

As you savor the joys of building and building more net worth, you will get more excited about your newfound abilities as time goes on and as net worth compounds and grows each year. Be sure you protect your growth with a good estate planning lawyer. Hire the best. You have worked hard to build your estate, so do not cut corners or deal with lawyers who are general practitioners. Hire only lawyers who have years of experience in estate planning matters. Travel the necessary distance to obtain the information that will help you and your family. If you like, you can call our Money and Marriage telephone number, 805-962-1040, and we will refer you to an attorney that is an expert in estate planning matters.

MANTRA

My daily actions will be parallel to and congruent with my goals and my financial plans for the future.

CHAPTER 9

Communication

The art of communication: some people have the knack for it and others have to learn this valuable relationship skill. Effective communicators know and understand both sides of the communication. They take responsibility for both sending and receiving messages to the other person. They make sure the other person understands what they are communicating and they also give the other person feedback so the other person is certain their words are being heard. It has been said that communication is one part speaking and two parts listening. This is why you have one mouth and two ears!

Effective active listening means you listen without interrupting, with genuine interest and without owning what the other person is saying. All too often in regard to money issues I hear a woman say she does not feel heard by her man. Effective communication in marriage is crucial. Here are key tips for better listening: 1. Give undivided attention. 2. Maintain eye contact. 3. Avoid interrupting. 4. Show empathy. 5. Reflect feelings. 6. Be patient. 7. Ask clarifying questions. 8. Avoid judgment. 9. Validate emotions. 10. Practice active listening daily.

When a woman says she wants to be heard, she is expressing a desire for her thoughts, feelings, and opinions to be acknowledged and respected. It means she wants others, particularly men, to *actively listen* to her without judgment or interruption. It often implies a need for validation, understanding, and equal participation in conversations. Being heard is a fundamental aspect of communication, ensuring that her voice and perspectives are given the attention and consideration they deserve.

Communication, emotional intelligence, and active listening are intertwined in effective interpersonal interactions. Communication involves conveying thoughts and feelings, while emotional intelligence enables understanding and managing emotions, both in oneself and others. Active listening, a key component of communication, involves attentive and empathetic listening to grasp the speaker's emotions and message fully. Emotional intelligence enhances active listening by enabling individuals to discern underlying emotions, fostering empathy and rapport. Together, these elements create a symbiotic relationship where empathetic active listening fosters better communication, and emotional intelligence enhances one's ability to interpret and respond to emotional cues, ultimately facilitating more meaningful and harmonious exchanges.

You hear about communication all the time. You must put communication into practice in your relationship. Communication is a skill. You will also need this skill in your business life. It is like two-for-one training. Train yourself to have good communication skills and you will be successful with your mate as well as your business staff, workers, contemporaries and banker. Your mate is the other essential person and the most important person in your life for you to demonstrate great communication skills with. You need to open your heart and let the other person in. You need to talk deeply, patiently and intimately on a regular basis.

Often emotional intimacy is confused with sexual contact. When I mention intimacy in consulting sessions, many people think you are going to talk about sexual topics. Instead, you need to become openly expressive with your mate about your emotions. Intimacy is the opening of yourself to the other, revealing yourself in order to provide the means for establishing the closeness, oneness, unity, bondng and connection with the person you desire. Intimacy is one of the most fundamental adult human desires. Intimacy provides the fusion in the relationship. Many people crave intimacy. This is part of how you get welded together and merge into one without losing your uniqueness, individuality and identity.

Communication intimacy between a husband and wife is the deep emotional connection and openness they share through effective and honest communication. From this comes trust. Communication intimacy involves the ability to express feelings, thoughts, desires, and vulnerabilities with one another without fear of judgment or rejection. This type of intimacy fosters trust, understanding, and empathy, allowing the couple to connect on a profound level. It enables them to navigate challenges, resolve conflicts, and support each other's needs and aspirations.

Communication intimacy is a cornerstone of a healthy and enduring marital relationship, enhancing the bond and promoting lasting love and connection.

Many couples who are clients say they have a good and intimate relationship. Usually after a few questions I find out they have great sex together, but they have very weak communication skills and practices.

Intimacy is not a skill people are taught in their parents' home or in schools while growing up. Intimacy may be very scary to people. They have to sit down and open themselves up to another person in such a way that it reveals who they are, what makes up their past, what they are doing presently and where they are going. Some people may not be consciously aware of what is going on inside themselves. If this is so, how are they going to explain it to someone else?

Your mate will find it very, very difficult to communicate with you if they do not feel safe in the relationship. When your partner is feeling safe, accepted and trusting of you in the relationship, they will then risk opening up to you. This starts the process of revealing yourself.

The most important thing you can do in your relationship is to dialogue with your spouse. You do not control his or her mind, body or actions. Both of you are unique individuals with very distinct direction, goals and financial goals, visions and needs. A criticism about men is that they often forget to ask a woman how she feels. To gain an understanding of how a woman feels, as well as how she thinks, is very important to your success with open, healthy communications.

There is no simple answer to why some men in married relationships may appear closed and unavailable for communication intimacy. It could be influenced by various factors, such as upbringing, societal expectations, personal experiences, or communication styles. Some men might struggle with expressing emotions due to cultural norms or fear of vulnerability, while others may have unresolved issues or stressors impacting their ability to connect. Effective communication and understanding between partners are essential to address such challenges and promote emotional intimacy within a marriage. It's important to recognize that these dynamics can vary greatly among individuals and couples.

Through dialoguing and open, healthy discussions, you are better able to gain an understanding of each other's needs, wants and desires. You can then prioritize these needs, wants and desires in developing your common family unit and team play goals.

The goal of dialoguing is gaining a perspective of the other's views. Because one spouse is a man and one spouse is a woman, believe me, your perspectives are distinctly different. The main mission of healthy dialoguing is understanding. Extra work needs to go into the understanding because of the profound differences between genders.

Communication intimacy should be evaluated in your relationship. Sexual intimacy is what has brought many couples together. Many couples can talk openly about their sexuality. They can tell the other partner what feels good to them and can guide their mate into some afternoons of pure pleasure ecstasy. If you are not there yet, there are many books about driving each other crazy in bed. I suggest you buy all of these books, because making progress with your sexual intimacy will open the gates for you to be more open and available with your communication intimacy.

In communication intimacy you reveal your secrets to your mate. You openly and honestly tell your mate all about yourself, your innermost thoughts and desires. Intimacy goes along with your willingness to be known and is coupled with feeling safe in the relationship and having a high degree of trust in your mate. Communication intimacy means dropping your social facade and exposing your true self. This means you have to disclose yourself, revealing your private thoughts and feelings. This involves taking risks. After venturing out and taking risks, you will feel greatly enhanced by the rewards.

The desire for intimacy is the desire to be thoroughly loved for who we are, not for who we appear to be.

Once you have played all of your cards, told all of your secrets and made full disclosure about yourself, there is a great feeling of relief that enhances your feeling of acceptance and makes that relationship bond much stronger. Your love for one another deepens, adding a new dimension to your relationship. All of this leads to becoming closer and more connected.

Again, you must evaluate and understand your fear structure. The fear of intimacy plays a part in all of this. You may be striving too much to be independent, anonymous and unique, to present your true face. You should be available to reveal the good, the bad and the ugly about yourself. Fear of intimacy exists because you have the fear of rejection, entrapment, commitment and loss of control, along with the dread of dealing with conflict that revealing yourself might bring about. You struggle with the dilemma of remaining private and on the other hand being close to someone.

Communication intimacy is the psychological basis for becoming a couple.

By understanding the need for communication and communication intimacy, you will be much more able to get together to set common goals toward financial independence. You will be much closer to joining your lives on a joint course, accomplishing the unity necessary to attain accomplishment and success.

Intimacy is very scary to some couples because they are required to open their private selves to each other. The innermost thoughts we share reveal who we are, why we do what we do, and where we are going. All of this is very important for your partner to know by hearing it from you. Your partner should not be required to figure out what is going on inside you. It is rare that I see a relationship that has a good mind reader. Often, however, there is a mate who is proficient in decoding nonverbal messages. You need to share your inner thoughts with your partner by using your words. Generally, for women all of this comes rather easy. Generally, a man would rather have you slice open his stomach with a kitchen knife without anesthesia than sit down and reveal himself. Thus, communication skills must be practiced over and over again. Practice makes it better.

Here is what in general women are looking for; they are looking for a stable relationship filled with warmth, trust, respect and under-standing. They want to be able to communicate with the person they love, tell each other the goodness in my heart, cry and laugh together, share the joys and sorrows of life together. When your man is having trouble sharing their feelings the woman should patiently want and with craft and diplomacy get out of the man their views and feelings topic by topic one and a time over a great deal of time. This way you can get what you want and enjoy the bliss of communication intimacy. The women in counseling that say well I don't understand way my husband can't just sit down and say his feelings? This woman obviously does not under-stand the concept of gender difference. To be blunt men and women access and speak about their feelings drastically differently.

Man and woman differences crop up when you talk about being in touch with your emotions. Generally, women are able to think and feel at the same time. This is like a double-duty computer, able to do two tasks at once: multitasking. Men, on the other hand, usually only think when they communicate. The man-woman (gender difference) differences are biological and cultural. This gives women an edge when it comes to interpersonal communications. Men respond to this by trying to over-power women with their words.

**To become intimate with your mate,
you must discover and know
your inner self.**

Let's take a look at communication with respect to how you would utilize communication to resolve conflict in an adult relationship.

Conflict in a relationship can be dealt with by better and more frequent communication. Conflict will be present because two distinct individuals are participating in the relationship. A conflict management system needs to be present so there is a civil way to move ahead.

Participating in arguments or conflict usually takes on these four forms. You either:

1. Plan to fight
2. Plan to flee
3. Plan to avoid
4. Plan to submit

Thus, we either explode or constrict our energy. Conflict can be either what fuels the relationship or, in most cases, what destroys it. Thus, some form of *conflict resolution system* needs to be put into effect. You need to develop a special signal or code when you want to take time to discuss important or troubling aspects of the relationship. Through active discussion and great communication skills, you can talk from the heart and spit out in words what is troubling you in the marriage relation-ship. Without frequent meetings for civil, quiet, from-the-heart discus-sions and the active exchange of information (with no penalties or retal-iation for topics brought to the surface), the relationship may be doomed before it gets started if intimacy is not allowed to enter and develop. You need to maintain these quiet times of active talking, communicating and listening. Without their continuance, a severe breakdown can occur.

Some form of conflict management system and conflict resolution system must enter the relationship.

If your spouse cannot open up and share personal thoughts and feelings about you or about themselves, if they have a great deal of trouble looking inside themselves, or if they always blame the other person, they are displaying symptoms that require immediate, professional counseling. These are the active signs that your mate cannot communicate intimately. Intimate communication skills are easy to learn and can relieve you of a lifetime of misery and struggle. Continue to note that this type of communication biologically comes easier for the woman than for the man.

Many people avoid conflict because they think that expressing their true feelings is going to be hurtful to the other person. This is a great fallacy in a relationship. Yes, you should be diplomatic. The timing, the setting, the tone of voice are all important factors. You cannot hold back your true feelings, though. They must be expressed out loud to your partner and must be expressed by you using your mouth, words and kind tone of voice. There is a rule learned when discovering how to become intimate with the person you love. The rule is that everyone has a right to their own feelings. You should be able to express your feelings out loud to your partner. The rule is that neither your partner nor anyone else can condemn you for your feelings. Your feelings are your feelings. Your responsibility in the relationship is to express your feelings in words out loud to the other person.

Relationship partners who maintain they have never fought, quarreled or argued are really in more trouble than they think.

In your relationship, you must have the positive feeling that you both have a legitimate right to feel and think the way you do. You must have the comfort of knowing that your feelings are valid and your partner actively listens and hears what your true thoughts and feelings are. Also, it is important to learn from each other and at the end choose what is most helpful in reaching your three and five-year goals.

You must make a binding pact to timely deal with your differences and conflicts in a way that is open, honest and loving.

Strong polarization for being independent and other chants of the women's movement have been very destructive to marriage relationships. Although you should feel free to express your thoughts and feelings, you should form them in the spirit of unity and teamwork focused on melding two people together for life. One learns that after airing your true feelings you may then both make adjustments to your prospective to better make a unified team.

Both parties have a strong desire to have their thoughts and feelings heard and to have their needs met.

Negotiation and compromise are your tools. Leave winning out of the picture. Attempts to win are destructive. Win/win conclusions, however, are a form of compromise.

It is relationship unsportsmanlike conduct to fake or make up a crisis only to say, "well now let's negotiate" this conduct is a destructive behavior.

Negotiation is going to play a part in your relationship. Within the relationship there are two people. There are bound to be differences, this is a certainty! These differences need to be resolved through a calm, methodical, reasonable method. Negotiation is a way to resolve differences. Negotiation is a form of intellectual Ping-Pong. Each side should have the opportunity to state their part, their thoughts, concerns, priorities and beliefs. The other side is obligated to enthusiastically listen, then at the appropriate time respond by first saying and summarizing the other party's statement to let them know that they have been heard. Then you can begin airing your feelings and stating their part. During negotiation, couples examine the differences in their core beliefs and priorities and attempt to develop a commonly held set of operating principles. Negotiation is difficult at first. Then you become better at it. Negotiation deepens your love, trust and respect for the other person and can heighten your passion for one another. Successfully getting through negotiation shows that you have become a couple and you are now able to work out the details in a civil and diplomatic way.

Negotiation is a process of communicating back and forth for the purpose of reaching a joint and mutual decision. When you negotiate, you are communicating and learning more and more about your mate. You must confront the issues and be willing to state your thoughts and feelings in order to resolve the matter. Part of negotiation is to quell anger in such a way that there is a calm open and honest discussion of the facts.

Rage, verbal abuse and anger should not be a part of your structured negotiation techniques. Sometimes, when you are interacting on a daily basis with all the stress of life about you, a discussion may reach the boiling point. This is when you need an agreed-upon code word that means "Let's stop, cool off and discuss the matter in our negotiation way."

You should consider a **code word** that means "Let's talk civilly." Naturally you should tell your mate right away what your code word is. The first lesson in negotiation is to agree on the same code word!

If you have difficulty arriving at a negotiating time and style, please consult a trained marriage counselor. They are equipped to show you proven techniques and format that will really work.

Anger is often not managed properly in the relationship. Avoid the syndrome whereby the husband yells at the wife and then the wife yells at the children.

Coming to know how, when and where to resolve your differences causes you to know and respect each other more deeply. You should learn a method that helps you both resolve conflict. This will cause your relationship, love and admiration for each other to mature and deepen.

Constructive criticism in a relationship is helpful when it is offered at the right time, in the right tone and in the right setting, with both parties providing a willingness to actively listen and then discuss.

Knock-down, drag-out arguments rarely produce beneficial results, but when they occur, making up has more passion. Unresolved arguments build up resentment and hostility. There is no way around this, it is much healthier to air it out, let out what is bugging you, don't let it fester. Compatibly resolving the conflict in the relationship can produce a sense of security.

It has been said in the movies that half the fun of having a fight is making up. The passion is definitely enhanced. Solid relationships usually do not need the fights to find the intensity. It is your choice.

Marriage goes fine through balance and communication. When conflict and difficulties set in, people seem to think the appropriate thing to do is change partners. Then they divorce, remarry and find the same problems resurfacing all over again. Rather than divorce and changing your partner, you might consider addressing and fixing the problem.

**Looking into the mirror for the solution may be of great
help to the stability of your relationships in life.**

The idea that you should just change partners when trouble or crises come is not a good one. You likely are a "flight" type of conflict resolver. Instead, you should recognize it is probably the way you are living with that person that should be changed. A conflict management system that works should be installed.

**Rather than getting rid of your spouse and
keeping the problem, you should get rid of
the problem and keep your spouse!**

Every relationship goes through daily, monthly and annual adjustments. As you age, your relationship has to have room for adjustment. As you grow and mature, your relationship must grow also. Relationships grow in stages that need constant discussion, negotiation and adjustment. Relationships survive when you make these adjustments together. If adjustments are not occurring, it is likely your partner will fight, take flight, avoid the issues or fold.

When negotiating with your spouse, remember who you are talking to. You are arguing with the love of your life, the person you vowed to spend the rest of your life with. When you are angry, get in touch with that love and begin with the phrase "I love you," then follow by stating how you feel. With the neutrality of a diplomat, state the facts that are happening that are causing your anger or upset. Have your partner repeat (mirror) what you have just said by beginning with the phrase "I hear that you are upset about...."

When your partner has finished, you can begin to ask for what you want. Listen and hear what the other person is able to give and strive to reach a win/win solution to the difficulty.

This can be broken down into steps of negotiation with your spouse.

Step 1
(Partner 1) Tell your partner you love them, even though you are not in touch with that feeling at that moment!

Step 2
(Partner 1) Tell them how you feel. "I feel sad, weary, helpless." Do not make a judgment statement. It has to be a feeling statement.

Step 3
(Partner 1) State the facts. Just the facts, like Joe Friday would want you to do. State the impartial facts as a newscaster would.

Step 4
(Partner 2) Repeat what your spouse (Partner 1) said by starting with, "I hear that you feel...." After repeating how the other person feels, stop.

Step 5
(Partner 1) Ask for what you want. Be reasonable!

Step 6
(Partner 2) Tell your partner how you feel about what they want. Then tell them what you will do to help them achieve a solution.

Step 7
(Both) Conduct a productive discussion by actively speaking and then actively listening when the other person speaks.

Step 8
(Both) Work toward a compromise resolution through quiet and active discussion.

Step 9
(Both) Repeat the agreement. Have your spouse repeat the agreement. Shake hands, hug, then do whatever.

You may want to put this set of instructions on the refrigerator. Make a pact to use your style of negotiation to resolve problems following your style of the steps. Use the above steps as a structural guide.

This exercise needs to be structured. You need to follow the flow of the structure. You can make it fun. In counseling so that one does not talk over the other person we use a tennis ball. The speaker hold the tennis ball and says their part but not to exceed so many minutes. Then the tennis ball is politely passed to the other person. They have the tennis ball and it is their turn to speak and the other person cannot interrupt even if the speaker pauses, as long as they are holding the tennis ball they are the only speaker. The ball continues to go back and forth until there is some form of compromise reached. This way no one can, very well anyway, control, manipulate, domineer the other person. Every one has a fair chance to speak for 8 minutes then ball is passed.

Often men do not know how they feel. Here is a list of feelings that may help you complete the sentence, "I feel...."

abandoned	embarrassed	overwhelmed
afraid	foolish	proud
angry	frightened	sad
ashamed	frustrated	satisfied
brave	glad	stressed
burdened	happy	threatened
courageous	horny	tired
depressed	indebted	woozy
disorganized	overjoyed	worried

Do not overlook the fact that occasional conflict is healthy and necessary in a relationship. For some conflict is what gives excitement to the relationship. Do not overlook the power that humor can have in resolving conflict. Light humor is a great healing agent. Too much humor during a serious discussion about your relationship is not good at all. Know you are taking all of these steps to reach that comfort zone of harmony and happiness for both sides in your relationship. Resolving conflict is what can take your relationship into the future without internal struggle. Be mindful of your joint three-year goals and your five-year goals and be sure that you resolve conflict in a way that brings you closer to meeting your 3-year and 5-year goals. Do not stray, be strayed or lose focus of the goal. More shopping or a bigger boat is not going to move you closer to meeting your goals.

Know that your partner has wants, needs, dreams and desires. Through compromise conflict resolution, see that you are meeting the wants, needs, dreams and desires of your mate. Prove from time to time that you *understand* the dreams, desires and priorities of your mate. If you do this, you will quite likely get more of what you want from the relationship.

Respect, consideration and kindness are things we give to our friends, employees and bosses. These qualities must be considered each day in our most important relationship. Learn to recognize, defuse, negotiate and resolve your conflicts in a loving way.

You should never threaten to end your relationship unless your partner does such and such. You should be striving to build a close, harmonious, closed-ended, *no-exit relationship*. Making a pact to do this might help. With a no-exit relationship, you both commit to resolving all differences within the relationship by using learned techniques to resolve conflict and struggle. The best, strongest and most fulfilling relationships are no-exit relationships. The challenges in your relationship often bring you closer together. Pledge to work through these challenges together. In dealing with these challenges, you are learning how to be a more diplomatic, expressive, communicative and articulate partner. Upset can be an opportunity for learning how to be a better relationship participant.

If you do not learn to resolve your differences, resentment will set in. Both sides will close out each other and the relationship will shut down. Then separation followed by divorce can occur. As a huge surprise to most men, divorce brings with it huge emotional pain, a kind of pain that most men and women have never experienced before. The pain of divorce is often described as emotional agony, affecting individuals deeply. It encompasses various forms of anguish, such as sadness, grief, anger, and even guilt. The depth of this pain can be profound, as it disrupts not only the marital bond but also one's sense of identity, security, and future. On top of this financial pain is the fact that the paid is administered by the court system.

A time for healing this pain is needed before you can do anything productively or successfully again. Time is the best medicine along with competent professional counseling, books, courses and new relationship partners.

Expect that this pain will bring about a type of paralysis that will make the most simple daily tasks very difficult to perform.

People have painfully discovered that divorce is not always the appropriate solution. Divorce can be devastating to well-laid net worth building plans. Divorce can be devastating to the children. To find someone new and train them to think in terms of building net worth can be quite difficult. Why divorce? You are just going to carry your bad relationship behaviors to the next marriage and then soon thereafter that will end in divorce! You should consider fixing the problems now and stay in the first relationship.

Many problems that come up in a marriage relationship are hinged around denial. The person giving off the problem is so sure they are doing the right thing that they cannot take an objective look at the marriage relationship and admit to themselves they need to make personal changes. Denial is a cornerstone in chemical and drug rehabilitation. More marriage rehabilitation facilities should be built to deal with the denial that exists in marriage relationships! If people could only see that their behavior is quite destructive to the marriage relationship, many of them would immediately stop the negative behavior or accept trained professional counseling.

People with this behavior are usually skilled in covering up and hiding their problems. They often tell you they could stop this negative behavior anytime they wanted to. In reality, though, they usually cannot.

If you can spot issues that come up in your relationship, you will be better equipped to supply the correct ointment or treatment.

Much the same as you keep a family medical reference handbook on the shelf for physical aches, pains, flus and fevers, you should keep a copy of this book on hand to deal with the financial and emotional aches and pains that are present in your household.

Note that when your spouse is physically under the weather, you usually fluff up their pillow and bring them hot tea and meals in bed. If your spouse shows signs of financial or emotional aches and pains, you usually become angry and want to argue with them. There is usually no compassion toward your spouse about their financial or emotional aches and pains. It seems like all the people involved only want to scream, yell and put you down for being in a weaker position than you were before. You feel verbally abused and emotionally battered, which adds to your "emotional illness."

Financial aches and pains can bring about many side effects. The people around you are not ready to fluff your pillow. Instead, they are ready to throw stones and hurl foul language your way. Financial aches and pains come from severe financial reversals. These reversals test your strength to regroup, gather your sense of survival and try something new in the marketplace.

In order to design something new, you need to tap into your creativity. But because of your emotional upset, your creativity is blocked. First a kind of paralysis sets in. Every task seems harder to do. Then you feel the effects of depression. In some people the effects of depression are more pronounced than in others. Next you are in an environment where your lenders, vendors, creditors and family are all being quite critical, or so it seems. During all of this you need to be ever so inventive and get something new going to stop the financial reversals.

If you have ever lost your job, felt the effects of a cyclical business or run a company that has been dealt a blow from changes in the marketplace, you can identify with the trouble described above.

If your spouse knew what was really going on inside you, possibly they would fluff your pillow rather than continue to ask when you are getting a new car, buying new furniture or going on a shopping trip.

Understanding comes from having excellence in communication skills.

You should learn to break this cycle and allow yourselves to cuddle and nurture the affected partner through the emotional and financial hurts they will undoubtedly experience.

In your marriage relationship, you may notice your spouse is having Sunday evening anxiety. Any spouse of a professional, an executive or someone in a high-stress job should be watchful for this well-known phenomenon.

Does your spouse act irritable and unapproachable on Sunday evenings? This is usually the case following two complete days off. If this is so, it needs to be responded to with kindness and understanding. What your spouse is experiencing is the dread or pressure that is awaiting them when it is "show time" on Monday morning at the office.

The two days off felt so good, and now the reality of the mountains that need moving tomorrow, the problems that need dealing with or the required competency level are confronting your spouse.

The best thing to do is to give your spouse some space. Know this is a bad time and allow your spouse to get ready to be a tiger tomorrow.

Some words of encouragement or a special thanks for all you do is especially good therapy.

There are many disorders that all people in a relationship should be aware of. This awareness will help you spot emotional illness or addictions that can save your finances and save your relationship. The following are some fairly common disorders that people might encounter in their families or in their relationships. You should find out more about these from a qualified professional if you suspect your mate may have a problem.

Learning disorders, such as dyslexia. These are sometimes spotted at an early age and sometimes in later life. A learning disorder could be one reason your spouse does not want to try another occupation.

ADD (Attention Deficit Disorder). This is more and more being diagnosed during school years. Surprisingly, though, some people do not discover they have a form of ADD until their careers are well underway.

Hyperactivity. This is sometimes controlled by drugs so people can enjoy a normal pace with their thoughts, actions and behaviors.

Medical issues:

cancer avoidance measures	sexually transmitted disease
exercise program	sleep management
heart disease management	smoking
high-fat diets	stress management
pregnancy management	weight management

Take the above list to your medical doctor and your nutritionist and have them explain each and every item. Have them explain how these relate to you and your relationship.

Emotional and mental issues:

addictions to alcohol, drugs, gambling
adjustments
ambitiousness
anger management
anxiety management
attitude
blaming the other
bonding
boundaries
child abuse—physical, sexual, emotional
closeness
codependency
compulsive behavior
conflict management
connecting
constructive criticism
contribution
control
depression
desire for abundance
discipline
eating disorders
ego
emotional health
energy management
enthusiasm

fear management
feelings
financial depression
helplessness
high demand
hug necessity
insecurity
intimacy
manipulation
mood swings
manic depression
neurosis
optimism
parenting decisions
parenting skills
personality
procrastination
punctuality
self-confidence
self-esteem
self-worth
sense of compliance
sense of order
sexual appetite
social personality
sociopath
trustworthiness

Take this second list to your marriage counselor and have them explain each and every item. Have them explain how these relate to you and your relationship.

Visiting with these professionals will move you closer to achieving excellence and becoming a unified, healthy, peak-performing unit.

Additionally in your relationship you will want to list, discover and further develop your spiritual connection. In dealing with your spiritual connection, if you have a certain way you connect with your higher power, please do everything possible to keep this going throughout your life. Find a place that is right for you to worship with people you feel connected to. Your spiritual side, when developed, provides the energy you will need to carry on during the week. Then go again the following week to refuel. Some people find their connection with their higher power through meditation or prayer. Whatever your spiritual connection is, be sure you keep it up. Be open to finding ways to increase your spiritual connection.

Mid-life crisis is real! Sometimes sound professional counseling can help. Most of the time you need to be helpful and understanding while time works to heal the person struggling with the difficulties that accompany this period. Mostly the turbulence comes from unresolved issues in one's childhood or from trying to understand the necessity for one's present-day existence. The only hope for the relationship during this period is that the spouse remains patient. The storm may take up to 36 months to blow over.

Mid-life crisis is known to hit anywhere from age 37 to age 44. This is a period in which I have seen successful people throw down everything and decide they have not done enough mountain climbing in Alaska, fishing in Montana or traveling in Europe. These people have walked away from the financial assets they have accumulated and decided they wanted to pursue something they think they are growing too old to do anymore. This can include the idea that they are getting too old to chase members of the opposite sex. Thus, they start fooling around while they are still married. This period is when the lake is turning inside the person.

In a lake at certain times of year, the bottom turns and comes to the top while the top is forced to the bottom. This is nature's way of keeping the lake healthy. Within humans, this process involves defining a person's existence and focusing one's direction.

Some people move through this mid-life period without much upset to the marriage relationship. Others do not. The important thing is to know of its existence. If your spouse all of a sudden wants to do something really weird that takes you off course from building net worth, you will know that possibly the mid-life crisis is beginning to play a part in your life. During this period your spouse's mental and emotional outlook may take some pretty wild turns. Spot the issue and know that usually this all blows over and happy net worth building and relationship building can resume.

Mid-life crisis comes from failing to resolve the issues confronting us. All of our frustration and disappointment come to a head in mid-life crisis, a desperate last-ditch attempt of the psyche to restore itself. The changes are so age inappropriate and disruptive that they can lead you to divorce all too quickly.

If you want your relationship to last for the long term, be aware of this very turbulent time in adult life. This affects men and women with much force.

When adults have unresolved issues from childhood and unresolved issues from their relationship, combined with the challenges of growing older, the feeling that life is passing them by and built-up desires. This causes seemingly normal, responsible people to make abrupt changes in their lives. Women have given up their children to go backpacking in Europe for an unknown duration. Spouses have walked out of the family businesses, gone home, packed their hiking boots and equipment and announced they are going to the mountains indefinitely, leaving the company and leaving the family.

Men and women who suffer from this phenomenon come back in a few years and wish they had never given up their marriage. This occurs when the self-righting adjusters in the brain find their balance once again. Many relationships have not been able to weather this storm. Note how many times divorce occurs within the age range of 37 to 44. Many people have awakened to find their financial assets carved up by attorneys and courts, then wonder why it all happened.

Our childhood experiences play a part in why we choose a particular partner. Choice is a very important part of relationship management. In evaluating our childhood, we can ask ourselves what we want from a relationship, and we can predict what kind of relationship we might have. You need to do some serious evaluation, either by yourself or with the help of a professional counselor. Find out in list format what you missed in childhood. Find out how and to what degree you were physically abused, mistreated, emotionally battered or overlooked. Find out how you deal with conflict. Get in touch with this. Then find a marriage partner who will compatibly fill the role of providing you with those things you did not have in your childhood, such as a kind and caring spouse!

We should choose people of similar upbringing and childhood experiences. These should be people with similarities in family, background and values. A match of this kind will be much easier on both of you. Mating for life with the wild thing that caught your eye, will propose a road of change and compromise with different values and priorities. Your vision of family life, parenting, building financial assets, spending money, vacations and desires for the future, should be considered. With a good match comes compatibility and less struggle to get focused on building net worth. You will spend less time in training your spouse not to wastefully spend all of the family's financial resources. When you marry someone with the same vision of the future, you are apt to go much farther much faster. This can happen if you make a good selection when you start the marriage relationship. Thus, there is a lot of importance placed on your choice of partner.

If you select a compatible match for your partner, you can save much frustration, pain and failure in your relationship. Instead, the joy, pleasure and contentment you have hoped for becomes a reality.

Everyone has a vision of their relationship and of the future. You need to consciously evaluate the issues and elements of a good relationship to fulfill your vision of the future.

In school we have had no training in communication, how to have relationships, or how to manage finances. Instead we were taught history, mathematics and science.

The object in successful negotiation is not winning, it is your ability to merge your set of goals and priorities into an end result of compromise. Change and adjustment are a normal and natural part of a relationship. This must occur if you are going to go into the future together.

Agree to adopt a method of communication that allows intimacy into your life. Use these methods to strengthen your ties together to create a bond that will last for life.

Know that your relationship will contain struggles, power plays and conflict. Adopt a problem resolution system that will work in your relationship.

Here are some important points to remember, as you build a long-term marriage relationship.

1. **Effective Communication:** Open, honest, and respectful communication is the cornerstone of a healthy marriage. Encourage couples to actively listen to each other's perspectives, as they learn how to express their feelings, and avoid defensive or confrontational communication styles. Avoid put downs. Hear the other side out.

2. **Empathy and Understanding:** Couples should strive to understand each other's emotions and perspectives. Teaching couples to empathize and validate each other's feelings fosters a sense of emotional connection.

    Successful married couples often exhibit a deep sense of empathy and understanding towards each other, particularly when it comes to acknowledging and navigating the emotional differences between men and women.

    Empathy forms the cornerstone of a healthy relationship, enabling partners to connect on a profound level. It involves actively listening and *validating each other's feelings*, regardless of gender, fostering a safe and supportive environment.

    Understanding men-women emotional disparities is crucial. Men and women often have different communication styles and ways of processing emotions. How women process their emotions is as different as night and day when compared to how men process their emotions. This difference has existed for more than 5,000 years. Recognizing these differences can prevent misunderstandings and conflicts. For instance, women may lean towards sharing their emotions openly, seeking connection, while men might be more inclined to process internally or engage in problem-solving. Note women don't need fixing they need someone to listen, help them feel understood, then validate their feelings. Then begin a process of putting the pieces together in real life and day to day household management.

    Successful couples embrace these variances, using them as opportunities to grow and complement each other. They prioritize open dialogue, aiming to bridge the emotional gap through patience and respect. By nurturing empathy, understanding, and an awareness of these differences, couples can create a harmonious and enduring partnership built on mutual love and acceptance with everyone feeling good.

3. **Conflict Resolution Skills:** Conflict is inevitable in any relationship when 2 people are involved! Families should equip themselves with effective conflict resolution strategies, first hear them out then emphasizing compromise and problem-solving rather than winning arguments.

4. **Quality Time and Connection:** Couples should spend quality time together, nurturing emotional intimacy. Couples should engage in activities and travel that promote bonding and shared experiences.

5. **Individual Growth:** A successful marriage allows space for individual growth and development. Couples should support each other's personal development and aspirations to build financial net worth.

6. **Managing Expectations:** Realistic expectations play a vital role in marriage. Couples should understand that perfection is unattainable, and there will be ups and downs. Couples should learn to cope and manage expectations this can reduce disappointments.

7. **Intimacy and Romance:** Couples should prioritize physical intimacy and romance in their relationship. Lean in the direction of new ideas, discovery and the habit of moving closer to becoming sexual athletes. Remember it is exchanged and shared pleasure, it is not a one-way street. Couples should know that maintaining a spark is not only healthy it is crucial for a long-lasting marriage. Good cardio exercise is important.

8. **Conflict Avoidance vs. Resolution:** Couples should distinguish between healthy conflict resolution and unhealthy avoidance. It's important to address issues rather than sweep them under the rug. Conflict avoidance in a marriage can have several negative consequences and potentially damage the

relationship over time. While avoiding conflict might seem like a way to maintain peace in the short term, it often leads to underlying issues festering and growing. Here are some of the potential damages that can result from *conflict avoidance* in a marriage:

Resentment: When conflicts are not addressed, feelings of frustration, resentment, and anger can build up over time. These negative emotions can erode the emotional connection between spouses. Pressure can build then suddenly one day the top blows off the top of the kettle.

Poor Communication: Points to poor communication skills. Conflict avoidance often means that couples don't effectively communicate about their needs, wants, desires, concerns, and feelings. This lack of communication can lead to misunderstandings, misinterpretations, and a breakdown in the overall quality of communication in the relationship.

Unresolved Issues: Over time, the lack of conflict or arguments harbors submerged, unresolved conflicts which accumulate, creating a backlog of unaddressed issues. This can make it difficult for couples to move forward and find solutions to ongoing problems.

Emotional Distance: As conflicts are avoided, emotional distance can grow between spouses. This can result in a lack of physical intimacy, closeness, and emotional connection within the marriage. Obviously, this is a couple moving in the wrong direction.

Escalation: In some cases, unresolved conflicts that are avoided may eventually reach a breaking/boiling point, leading to explosive arguments or even the threat of separation or divorce. The poor communicator, conflict avoider, when they blow up, they can run for divorce rather than face the issues and restore and rejuvenate the marriage.

Lack of Growth: Healthy conflict resolution can lead to personal and relationship growth as couples work together to find solutions and compromise. It is a method of carefully letting it all out. Conflict avoidance can hinder this growth by preventing couples from learning how to navigate challenges together.

Loss of Trust: When one or both partners consistently avoid addressing issues, it can lead to a loss of trust. Trust is huge and quite essential in any relationship, and when conflicts are avoided, it can be difficult to trust that your partner will be there to work through problems with you.

Impact on Emotional Well-being: Living in a constant state of unresolved tension and conflict avoidance can take a toll on the emotional well-being of both partners. It can lead to stress, anxiety, and even depression.

It's important for couples to find a healthy balance between conflict avoidance and conflict resolution. It is not necessary to deal with conflict daily or on any particular schedule. While it's not necessary to engage in every disagreement with a full-blown argument, at the appropriate time and setting it is crucial to address important issues, express feelings, and work together to find solutions. Healthy communication, active listening, and the willingness to compromise can help couples navigate conflicts in a way that strengthens their relationship rather than damaging it. If conflict avoidance has become a pattern in your marriage, seeking the assistance of a couple's counselor can be beneficial in learning healthier ways to manage conflicts and improve the overall quality of your relationship.

9. **Seeking Professional Help:** Normalize the idea of seeking couples counseling when necessary. Sometimes, external guidance can provide valuable insights and tools to navigate challenges. Good counselors have the tools and can show you how to have conflict, exchange ideas, hearing the other person all the way to the end and then move on to mop it all up with some kind of mutually comprised and understood plan going forward.

10. **Adaptability:** Highlight the importance of adaptability as couples grow and change over time. Encourage them to embrace change together rather than resisting it.

The key to a long-term, successful marriage lies in effective communication, empathy, conflict resolution skills, tolerance and a commitment to nurturing the relationship. By addressing these pieces of the puzzle, family marriage counselors can help couples build enduring and fulfilling long term marriage.

With all the stress of daily life, remember to send your beloved a love note. Weave in some of these words into your note to send the sincere, humorous or playful, message of love and romance and remind your spouse that you truly love them. Hand written notes are the best, automatic email messages are not believed as authentic or sincere! For the women flowers work wonders, for the man?? A beer, kiss or cigar, candy?? A woman's intuition will know!

- Beloved
- Sunshine
- Enchanting
- Graceful
- Radiant
- Passionate
- Admiration
- Sparkling
- Dreams
- Inspiring
- Strength
- Beautiful
- Captivating
- Empowerment
- Cherished
- Queen
- Success
- Resilience
- Elegance

- Alluring
- Devotion
- Spark
- Magical
- Brilliance
- Affection
- Ambition
- Glowing
- Dazzling
- Heartfelt
- Fortune
- Endearing
- Loveliness
- Achievement
- Devotion
- Charisma
- Gratitude
- Triumph
- Enthusiasm
- Glamour
- Happiness

MANTRA

I commit daily to being the most proficient, open and honest communicator with my spouse.

CHAPTER 10

Financial Investments

There are many important financial decisions you are going to have to make during your lifetime. Let's spend some time reviewing some of the more important financial investments you will make in your financial future.

Please know and understand that each married couple will have to address these decisions together. Previously we have seen that there are many man and woman differences when it comes to making decisions. Men and women have different methods of gaining perspective and different sets of priorities. In order to make these decisions, you need to actively discuss and merge your ideas together. You should not feel that the man makes all of the decisions and you have to live with them. You should not feel you have to acquiesce to all of the woman's concerns. You need to gain the feeling you are working as a team. You need to come to mutual agreement, jointly through active discussion, to decide how, when and to what degree you will make these financial commitments.

Achieving mutual agreement in financial discussions between men and women involves acknowledging and bridging gender differences. Start by fostering open communication to understand each other's perspectives, values, and priorities. Recognize that differing outlooks may stem from societal conditioning and past experiences. Encourage compromise and find common ground by seeking shared financial goals. Establish clear financial objectives and boundaries, and consider seeking professional financial advice when needed. Ultimately, mutual respect and empathy for each other's viewpoints can help bridge gender-related disparities and pave the way for more harmonious and equitable financial decision-making.

In other parts of the book, we discussed the investments you must make by putting your career earnings into common stocks, bonds and mutual funds and ETF's. Now we will discuss the major financial investments you will encounter in your lifetime.

You are going to need the help of some professional people. You will need a banker, attorney, insurance agent, CPA. stockbroker, mutual fund company, business broker, real estate broker and marketing advisor. You are going to need periodic reference to financial newspapers and magazines. The *Wall Street Journal* and *Investors Business Daily* should be close at hand. You can find these at your local library or online. You will need some magazines such as Business Week, Money, Forbes, Fortune, INC, Entrepreneur and Success.

KNOW THY BANKER WELL

Your banker can be quite helpful to your financial success. Heed this message about the importance of knowing your banker well. The banker sees many different financial situations during the year. All of this experience can help you prosper. Let the banker into your inner circle, let the banker be your friend. Meet the highest official at the bank, for example the bank branch manager or the overall President for a local or regional bank.

The bank you choose is important. Choose a bank that has a banker you want to work with, a person who is knowledgeable and can be your friend, advisor and confidant. Your banking relationship is going to be important to your investment life. Your banker can greatly assist you in establishing the correct type of accounts within the branch. You want to groom the relationship with your banker to become eligible for certain privileges. Ideally you would like to have the greatest reduction of service charges. You would naturally want to earn the highest interest income possible on your bank accounts. You would like to have your accounts free of restriction. You will need to arrange for overdraft protection.

You should maintain most of your monies with your primary bank. Look for openings of new local banks that offer free checking accounts. Look for banks that offer compounded interest paid daily.

Be certain your bank pays interest daily and the interest is compounded daily so at the end of the month you are earning the most you can. Many people today use a money market mutual fund or their stock brokerage account to accomplish this goal.

Your bank will charge you fees. There could be fees each time you deposit, write a check, bounce a check, use the ATM, use someone else's ATM, transfer money or take out a loan. There may be a monthly fee for each account you have, and fees if accounts go below an agreed minimum balance. Be observant of the fees and ask your banker to help you build your net worth by keeping to a minimum the fees they are charging you. Your banker will be so happy to hear that you are earnestly trying to build your net worth that you should have little trouble gaining their cooperation.

Some banks charge a fee if you get your cancelled checks or check images returned to you at the end of each month. If you are self-employed, you really want to have all of your cancelled checks returned to you. You should explain to the bank that you are self-employed and you want to keep good records for tax reasons. Your cancelled checks or check images are part of keeping good records. You also may want your cancelled checks to show proof of making a payment should a vendor or lender make posting errors.

Often the taxing authorities do not record or give credit for all of your estimated tax payments. You will want your cancelled checks to show proof. The back of any check paid to a governmental agency has numbers, dates and codes that will be very helpful in proving you deserve full credit for payments you have made.

Some banks offer overdraft protection. You should subscribe to this program. Overdraft protection will help save you the embarrassment of a returned check. It will reduce the amount of fees the bank charges for bounced checks. Discuss this matter with your banker. You should have such good managerial control over these accounts so that you never have to use overdraft protection.

If your spouse tends to overdraft the account, you might set up a fine fund that the offending party has to make a deposit into. Each time there is an overdraft, the offending party has to pay the family a fine. Use the fine fund for something silly or special that the whole family will enjoy.

Some banks offer you insurance services and offer to help you make financial investments. Some banks have a private banking department.

Know that your banker is there and really wants to help you build net worth. Your banker wants to be your friend. You must take the first steps in getting acquainted with your banker. If you are self-employed, you will want to bank with a commercial lending institution. Ask around in your community for a list of banks that are helpful to people in business. You want to establish your banking relationship with a bank that is capable of providing you with a line of credit to be used in your business.

Some banks have trust departments. If you want your money or your estate managed, you can appoint the bank trust department. You can do this during your lifetime or in your will or revocable living trust.

The benefits of using a bank trust department are that it is well insured and has assets to protect your assets. They have experience and act in an impartial way with some specialized knowledge.

During your lifetime or by way of your will, you can hire family members or independent businessmen you know and trust to be your trustee. Attorneys, lawyers and other businessmen may be a good selection, or a committee of all of these may be the way to administer your affairs. Some of these people might not have the insurance or the capital to allow your heirs to sue in the event of poor decisions, but they might be good businesspeople who can make business decisions swiftly and profitably.

Some bank accounts are insured and some are not. If you have over $240,000 in any one bank, you want to ask your banker about the federal insurance programs to see if you are covered. Government guaranteed programs will pay you back if you are in alignment with the qualifications. Know they will not pay you back very fast if the institution were to fail, but they will pay you back.

Some brokerage firms and insurance companies also offer insured accounts. Be sure you know who will be paying the insurance money should the brokerage firm or insurance company fail. It has been popular to advertise that your account is insured. It is shocking to find out that a firm could be insuring itself. Know the credit worthiness of the person providing the insurance. If the brokerage firm is insuring itself, know that if the firm is in financial trouble there is little chance there will be any real insurance money around to pay you. Be careful and keep asking questions until you have clear answers. Be certain you have written proof of the insurance and how and when it will be paid. Most institutions have a brochure about this.

Consult your banker often to obtain ideas on how you might better organize your accounts within the bank. Ask your banker how the bank can be helpful to your business. Ask your banker what records and documents they would like to see on a timely basis to enable you to keep your loans in place and easily renewable. Sit with your banker and make some goals for your business that would give it some financial strength. Banks as a whole could do a great service in helping people build net worth. Do not overlook you chance to establish an IRA account to get a tax deduction or strategically a Roth IRA account.

CREDIT CARDS

Inquire with your bank about the features of the credit cards they offer. There are many mainstream, low interest rate, low annual fee cards in the marketplace. Some card providers offer incentives, discounts, bonus points and/or mileage accumulations. Be sure to be aware of the cost of the annual fee and that interest rates may vary from 12% to 29% be alert to these important costs. Investigate all of the options thoroughly. Select the most economical one for you. Choose the card that is the least expensive, has zero or low interest charges and offers the most benefits. Credit card management requires that you use your credit cards in a responsible way.

With credit cards, be sure to pay off the entire balance at the end of every month. This will boost your credit score. For security reasons against hackers and card readers at your gas station, do not allow anyone to issue you a credit card that has more than a $4,500 credit limit, unless special circumstances exist. Always plan to have a low balance limit on your card. If you need more credit on the card, make a payment to the company in advance of your need for credit.

If you have a mainstream credit card, you can reduce your need to have a bunch of credit cards from retail stores because these stores always take mainstream credit cards. Having one card will help you manage then control the monthly commitments you have made. This will keep you from entering the realm of credit card abuse. Many married people struggle about the proper use and management of their credit cards. You should form mutual agreements about how much unpaid balance you will allow on you credit cards in total. Know that in marriage there is usually one person that keeps a zero unpaid balance and the other person may have secret credit cards and then allow the unpaid balance to soar. So periodically there should be a put all of your cards on the table meeting!

Avoid credit card abuse.

More people get into big financial trouble by abusing their credit cards. This happens very frequently. It can happen to young, old, educated or not-so-well-educated people. When asking these people why they got into this situation, often they do not know. Many of them are in denial that they are unable to utilize their credit cards in a non-abusive way. You need to have within your financial plans a program and pact that will not allow credit card abuse.

In our seminars we tell you ways to productively use credit cards to increase your investment holdings. Some strategies that have been used to purchase real property are also conveyed.

The use of credit cards can be damaging and destructive to the family unit and to the relationship you are daily building with your partner. Make a pledge to each other that you will employ modern techniques of "plastic surgery" on each other's cards if abuse becomes chronic. This requires a healthy discussion followed by full and honest disclosure about all of your credit cards.

CHILDREN'S SAVINGS TAX SHELTER

Savings accounts can be opened in the names of your children by using their Social Security numbers. The interest earned would be taxed to them. Basically, each child can have $10,000 in savings before they have to pay income tax at a high rate. If you have more than one child, each of them can have $10,000 in savings and not pay tax at a high rate.

CREDIT REPORTS

Before you make a real estate, investment or apply for a significant loan of any kind, you need to check your credit rating by examining the information contained in your credit report. To receive your credit report, write or go to the web site of the three major credit reporting agencies. These are:

Experian
Post Office Box 2104
Allen, Texas 75013
888-397-3742
www.experian. com

Equifax
Post Office Box 740241
Atlanta, Georgia 30374
800-685-1111
www.equifax.com

Trans Union
Post Office Box 1000
Chester, Pennsylvania 19022
800-888-4213
www.transunion.com

These are the three sources of mainstream credit reporting. Most banks subscribe to a service that gives them credit information about you from all three agencies. You need to inquire with each agency. Your credit might be clear at two agencies and all messed up at the third. Sometimes by using the addresses above you might be referred to a branch of the organization that is closer to your hometown. Be sure to follow through with making an annual inquiry with all three agencies.

It is important to make inquiry annually with all three agencies. Should any of these reports contain incorrect information, you can have the information deleted from your report by contacting the company. If the company cannot come up with proof of the accuracy of the information on the report within 30 days of your letter describing the incorrect information, they must then, on day 31, remove the information from your report. Credit reporting agencies sometimes break federal law and refuse to remove the information.

If they do verify the information in the report, you can require the credit reporting agency to label that debt entry on your report as disputed. With disputed items, you are allowed to insert up to 100 words in the report that explain what the problem is. You will want to do this so the next prospective lender who receives a copy of the report has the opportunity to see that the matter is disputed and that a legitimate complaint exists.

Many times, you can contact the company that has provided the negative information to the agencies. If they value your future business, they may figure out a way to remove the negative information from your report.

Often you will find strange entries on your report that you did not make. There will be entries from companies you have not done business with. This happens because the credit reporting agency has you mixed up with someone else. If you have a fairly common name, this can be a fairly common problem. You may be Jon Smith, and the information for John Smith may be in your report. Once you present your identification, the agency must make this correction immediately.

Usually after seven years the information in your report must be dropped by the credit reporting agency. If you have items that are negative in your report, you can insist that the agency delete them from your report after seven years.

The Fair Credit Reporting Act is the federal law that credit reporting agencies must follow. You will be successful in suing these companies for the damages equal to your lost profits from investment opportunities if they do not clean up your report. You should, at least once per year, examine your credit report for its correctness. These companies need to be sued more often so they will remember to be more accurate in their reporting habits and less belligerent about making corrections and changes.

One strategy that helps keep your credit report in great shape is to know the credit cards and other loans that are reporting to these credit agencies. Some credit extenders do not report your payment timeliness to a credit reporting agency. But for those that do, be sure your monthly payment is prompt and on time, if not ahead of schedule. You should see that your payments are sent off routinely each month ahead of the posted due date, so there is no opportunity for these credit extenders to show a late payment on your credit report.

Everyone should strive to have a Triple A credit rating. With good financial management skills, you can have a Triple A credit rating. Should you have a late payment, you are allowed to post an explanation in the credit reporting file as to why the payment was late. The credit reporting agency must include your statement or explanation each time it prepares a report for a potential lender.

Do not be surprised to find incorrect information in your file. As mentioned above, someone by the same name or similar name may be reported in your file. You need to have this information immediately removed. Family member information may appear on your report. This is wrong and should be corrected immediately. All other such errors should be immediately corrected by the credit reporting agency.

Damages may be collected from the credit reporting company by filing a claim in small claims court. Consult your attorney for larger damage claims.

Your request for a report will cost between $8 and $15 each time, unless you have been recently turned down when applying for a credit card or other credit. If you have been turned down, you are eligible for a free copy of your credit report. Merely contact the credit reporting agency and provide them with a copy of the rejection letter. The credit reporting agency must then give you a free copy of your report.

Should you have rental properties, you would want to join the credit reporting agency's membership program. Then you can directly obtain information about your new applicants before they occupy your property.

Keeping your credit report clean will greatly assist you in obtaining new loans for future real estate investments. The best way to drive up your credit score is to get 3 or 4 credit cards. Make charges on the credit cards during the month. At the end of the month absolutely pay off the outstanding balance. Do this for 10 months and then check you credit score. Many banks offer to their customers free credit scoring information. Watch for their offers and sign up or ask your branch manager if the bank offers such a program and sign up at the bank managers direction.

BUYING YOUR HOME

Before buying a home reread the communication chapter with your spouse. We have recommended that both husband and wife have a copy of this book and the women can underline in pink and the men can underline in blue and after reading switch books. Both will be surprised to learn what the other person considers important.

Before buying a home together you will really want to know your partner. Have a discussion about the projected costs of home ownership. Who is going to be responsible to pay for the related costs of home ownership? The commitment monthly to; the mortgage payments, the property tax, the insurance, the repairs, the improvements and the furnishings. Don't financially burry yourselves in house. Purchase a house with eyes wide open. Buying a home is a very exciting process. When you set out to buy a home, all kinds of things are happening physically, emotionally and mentally. Everyone is getting excited.

Buying a home provides shelter for your family and a shelter from paying income taxes. For years, the government has promoted and encouraged home ownership by allowing an income tax deduction for interest paid and property taxes paid.

Buying a home is very helpful in building your net worth. The home is usually the first big financial investment that a family makes. As you build equity, you build net worth.

You want your home to be a sound investment.

I cannot tell you how many times a person has interrupted a seminar to correct me on this point. They suggest that it is nearly inhumane to think so clinically about "their home."

If you can gather yourselves, you need to understand that your home must be a sound investment. This is difficult because most real estate offices are all set up waiting for you. Your professional Realtor can be very helpful to you. Ask around your friends, your banker and find a Realtor that is a match and works well with you. Realtors know that the home is an emotional buy and they stand ready to help you through the process. People often are not thinking right when they buy a home. They are strictly running on emotion and rarely do they come prepared with their investor hat on.

People who sell real estate do so all year long. When you go to buy a house, you may only do so once or twice in your life. Be sure you are ready for this experience. Do not become a statistic. Start out well-informed about the real estate market in the area in which you plan to buy a home. Be armed with information, and be ready to make good, sound, financially rewarding decisions. Know if you are buying a home in a buyer's market or a seller's market. Find out about troubled properties in your area.

Evaluate the area. Know the current and forecast real estate economic conditions. Know if any employers in your area are scheduling a large layoff soon. Know if any economic conditions are going to have a high impact on your market area. These can be conditions that are in your favor or not in your favor. Make a chart of houses in your desired price range. Know their price five years ago. Know their price ten years ago. Know their price fifteen years ago. Go down to the county offices in your area. Do research on any home you plan to make an offer on. If you are a good researcher, you can find out what the seller of the property paid for the house and the year they bought it. You can find out exactly the year when the house was built. You can find out how many times the house has been sold and for what prices. If you are good then all of this information is online in various websites. How many days has the home been on the market. What are the total square feet of the house, not including the garage.

Avoid having your home be an emotional buy.

Buy your house as a good investor would. You want to make a deal at the best price. Search out those good deals. Make reasonable and sometimes low offers. Be ready to walk away from the property if your offer is not met. If you do not play back-and-forth games with the seller, you will earn their respect and they will know you are educated and serious buyers. Know that in real estate many times the majority of the profit is made by purchasing the property at a greatly reduced purchase price. There are many reasons that a great property will be offered at a significantly reduced price. You need to know how to hunt for and find these properties. Often you will discover them on your own. You want to make a profit in buying your home. Your best hope in making a profit is to lock a good profit in on the buy side of the transaction. A large part of the ultimate profit can be made by how well you buy the property.

This is not to say that the home should not have all the function, features and amenities you are looking for. It should. By the way, do not buy a house that does not have all of the function, features and amenities you are looking for or that cannot have them added on in a short period of time.

A rule of thumb is to stay far away from a house that is advertised as a "fixer-upper." You might buy a house and fix it up, but never buy a house advertised as a fixer-upper, because they may need too much fixing!

Read between the lines. Know in advance how frustrating buying a house can be. Do not succumb to the process. Relax, take your time hunt, shop and buy as a good investor would. Find the right house, at the right price, at the right time for you.

When a husband and wife are buying their first house, common errors often include insufficient financial planning, such as underestimating the true cost of homeownership. Another mistake is not conducting thorough research on the housing market and neighborhood, leading to potential buyer's remorse or unexpected issues. Failing to get pre-approved for a mortgage can also hinder the buying process. Poor communication between spouses regarding their preferences and priorities can lead to disagreements during the home search. Overlooking the importance of a home inspection may result in costly surprises after purchase. Effective communication, financial preparation, and diligent research are crucial to a successful homebuying experience.

A Realtor is invaluable to homebuyers in several ways. They possess extensive knowledge of the local real estate market, providing insight into neighborhoods, pricing trends, and property values. They save buyers time by identifying suitable listings, arranging viewings, and handling paperwork. Realtors negotiate on behalf of buyers, securing the best possible deal and terms. Their expertise helps navigate the complex buying process, from inspections to financing. Additionally, they often have a network of contacts, including lenders and inspectors, streamlining the entire transaction. A Realtor's guidance and experience are instrumental in making informed, successful homebuying decisions. Know there is opportunity to work with a Realtor that represents the seller and you can also engage a Realtor to be the buyers broker, representing your position is their first importance.

Once you are in the home, be careful not to get caught up in what we call in our office the "doctor syndrome." This is where you buy a house and then commence making your mark on the property by adding things on and changing things a bit. For example, I have seen people buy a house for $300,000 and put $200,000 of additional improvements into the property: spas, landscaping, stereo systems and automated and electronic gizmos everywhere. Later they calculate that they have put a total of $500,000 into the house, which, having been in an upward growth market the entire time, can now you find out from an appraiser that your house now that it is fixed up will sell in the open market for $375,000. Folks, this is not good business or investment planning.

The home is a special sanctuary. You need to have the home that is appropriate for you.

Plan to buy a house that by way of purchase price and appreciation will provide you profit from the transaction. Don't get in over your head in your new house. Do the financial numbers and planning in advance of closing escrow.

Know that the real estate market moves in a cycle. The market goes up and the market goes down.

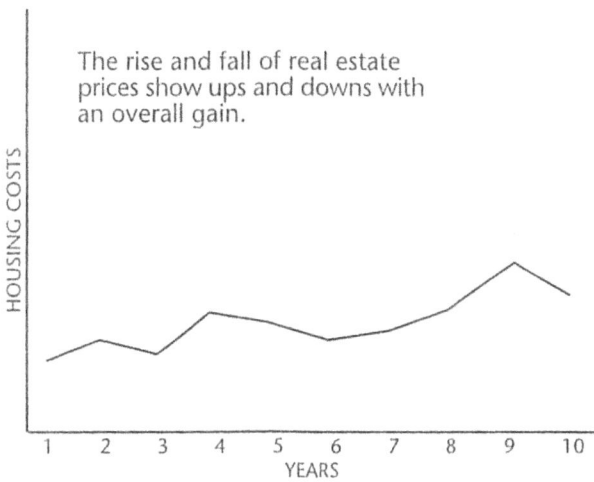

The rise and fall of real estate prices show ups and downs with an overall gain.

HOUSING COSTS

YEARS
1 2 3 4 5 6 7 8 9 10

You do not want to buy high and sell low. This, too, is not good investment planning. Know the cyclical movements of the market. Know whether or not you are in a buyer's market or a seller's market. This will help you see that you might get caught buying at the very top of the market and quarterly watch the value of your house decline. This does not help sprout happiness.

Whenever you buy a house, have a home inspection service thoroughly look it over. If you cannot locate a home inspection service, have a licensed general contractor become the inspector. Make sure they were not the builders of the home. Make sure they give you an unbiased list of the house's good and bad points. Before the inspection is started, have the seller give you copies of the last six months of utility bills from all service and utility providers. This will be important information for you and for your home inspector. Be sure the home inspection evaluates the capacity and output of the heating and air conditioning system. Does the plumbing have copper pipes or plastic pipes? When was the roof last installed?

If the seller will not provide this information, be tipped off that something is not right with what they are telling you, about the property and the costs of operating it.

Do not be alarmed when the inspection service has you sign a long contract saying they are not going to be responsible for anything. This is normal. These companies have been threatened by lawsuits so many times that they have some pretty forgiving contracts.

Be certain that the big items are carefully inspected: the roof, foundation, fencing, electrical, heating, air conditioning, plumbing and appliances included in the transfer. Find out the year of installation of each of these. Find out in advance how many more years they are expected to last. If you are a good negotiator, the list of problems from the inspector can be handed to the seller. You then tell the seller you will be available to buy the house when all the repairs are completed. Another way is to have these repair costs be added into escrow to lower your purchase price and you will over time make the repairs and the rest of the deferred maintenance.

Raise questions: has the seller had any claims with their home insurance company in the last five years. Check on previous water damage and check on the mold issues within the home.

Normally the home inspection is not started until the buyer and seller have agreed upon all of the terms of the sale, including a firm agreement on the purchase price for the home. All of these terms and conditions are conditional and will not become firm until the home inspection has been completed and the buyer has accepted the home with all of these observed defects.

If you plan to build a home, be careful. This can become your worst nightmare or your most fun and rewarding experience. One thing is certain: you will end up over budget for the house. At the end you will be very proud of what you were able to build.

Home building puts an incredible strain on your relationship. You become acutely aware of man-woman differences. There are thousands of building decisions to be made, and you need to make all of them together. This will test your relationship like no other endeavor in your lifetime. I cannot tell you how many couples have decided to divorce after building a house together. Be aware of this factor. No one else is going to tell you about this problem with home building. Building a home will put an incredible strain on your relationship. Only those couples with strong relationships fibers will survive the experience of building a home together. Why jeopardize your relationship?

In buying a home, you want to commit no more than 33% of your net take-home pay to house payments. In some areas known for rapid appreciation in the real estate market, it is safe to venture out a little more. If your market is going to appreciate rapidly in the near future, you may be able to expend up to 38% of your net take-home pay for home mortgage payments. This begins to tell you how much of a loan you will qualify for.

If you are just starting a business, it is very difficult to purchase a home within its first five years. If you buy a home, you may be diverting the necessary extra cash you need to invest in the business. You may be setting yourself up for financial disaster. Be careful and thoroughly discuss your ambitious plans with your spouse. Both of you need be on the same page, support each other and have the same understanding about the commit and the sacrifice ahead when you first purchase a home.

If you have transferred to a new area or taken a job in a new area, it is wise to rent until you are certain the new job is going to work out for you. You need to buy and hold a home usually for at least four years before you can earn a profit worth your while. You need to know the market conditions in the area where you are buying. Be certain you know which school district will serve your children. You need to know this for your children and also the children of the parents to whom you will sell your home. Always buy a home in the popular school district if you are under 40 years of age.

When you move to a new area, renting for a while allows you to get comfortable with the town. You gain a sense of whether the new job is going to work out for the long term. Many people who move to a new area soon learn that the job is not working out. They get caught with the market turning down, too, and learn they must sell their home at a loss. You need to avoid this circumstance.

Also, as a general rule, you will have to own the house for a couple of years for the market to appreciate enough so you can sell at a profit after you pay the closing fees and commissions and the other expenses of selling the property. You always want to prepare a "do we rent or do we buy" analysis on paper to help you see the true costs of home ownership. Market timing to your entry into the real estate market is quite important.

FINANCING YOUR HOME

In financing your home, there are a number of strategies that would allow you to buy your house with little or no money down. When you do get the main loan for your house, a good strategy would be to negotiate the loan so it is no more than a 30-year loan. Get the 25- or 30-year loan, but make a commitment together to pay it off in 15 years by making monthly principal reduction payments. Make sure when you sign the documents for the loan that the lender does not penalize you for making extra monthly principal reduction payments.

If you pay off the loan in 15 years, you will save a substantial amount of money. The full payment from year 16 through year 30 is saved. For example, if your monthly payment is $1,000 and you pay off your loan at the 15 year rate, you will save $180,000 over the life of the loan. This is computed as $1,000 x 12 months x 15 years equals $180,000. The period of time from year 16 through year 30 is 15 years. If you pay off your loan at the 15-year rate, you pay small dollars today to save big dollars tomorrow. The extra amount you pay each month to have the loan paid off in 15 years is not very much. You want the 30-year loan in case you have a couple of tough months and cannot make the extra principal reduction payments those months. With the 30-year loan, you will have the flexibility to decide what months you want to make the extra principal reduction payments.

Look into this opportunity with a pad of paper and a calculator at hand. See the large amount that can be saved in the future by making a little larger principal payment today. This savings is there in every home. Only the wise take advantage of this savings opportunity. You should check with your lender to find out what the 15-year loan payment would be. The lender is all set up to tell you this amount. They have books, calculators and amortization tables. It is very easy for them to provide you with the information.

Another approach that will accomplish a similar result would be to pay monthly an extra $100 per $100,000 of mortgage you have. Thus if you have a $300,000 mortgage, you would pay an extra $300 per month as a principal reduction payment. In the tough months don't make the payment. If you stick to this program, you will pay your mortgage off early and save thousands of dollars in payments in the last 15 years of the 30-year loan.

Note that some lenders require you to pay additional sums into a special account they maintain called a mortgage escrow account. This account has nothing to do with your extra payment to reduce the principal of your loan.

The escrow account may be required by your lender to allow the lender to be in control of funds to pay the fire insurance premium and property taxes on your property. It is helpful to the lender to extract these extra funds from you because they can then be certain that the fire insurance is maintained and they will be paid in the event of fire. They can also be certain that the property taxes are paid so the local tax collector does not sell the property to collect the property taxes. If you can convince your lender that you are disciplined and are financially responsible, they may waive the requirement for the escrow account. As you build equity in the property, the decision to waive these requirements may become easier for your lender to make. Some states require lenders to pay you interest on the escrow funds until they are paid out to an insurance company or tax collector. In states that do not require interest to be paid, understand that you can ask your lender to pay you interest on these funds.

You should annually track the actual charges to cover the insurance premiums and tax costs and compare this to what your lender has collected from you and paid. Always monitor the money in the escrow account and call any questions or discrepancies to the attention of the lender.

You also need to keep a separate and accurate record of your principal reduction payments. Compare monthly the amounts your lender has attributed to principal. Make sure you have been given credit for the appropriate amount. As good businesspeople, you need to keep these records and compare your records to your lender's summary.

When you negotiate your loan, you will have to make a lot of choices in a short period of time. All of the documents you will have to sign are presented in page after page of fine print. You need to be certain you completely understand all of the requirements, responsibilities and terms contained in the loan documents. Do not accept a loan that has a prepayment penalty included. Be sure to print out, read and have had explained to you all points of a contract before you use electronic means to sign a contract.

You will likely have to choose between a fixed rate loan and a variable rate loan. With the fixed rate loan, you will have the same interest rate over the life of the loan. For the next 30 years you are sure what your payment will be. The minimum monthly payment will be the same over the life of the loan. The fixed rate loan is usually priced higher (interest rate is higher) than the numerous variable rate loan programs that your lender might present. If you like the known and do not like surprises, you should consider the fixed rate loan, provided the rate is 7% or less.

There are many factors to consider with a variable rate loan. It may seem like you will pay less per month. This is because a lot of variable rate loans have "teaser rates" included. The first year the payment is less and then you are off to the races. With the variable rate loan, your minimum monthly payment will go up and down over the life of the loan. Your minimum loan payment could rise each year and eventually increase your monthly payment to an amount that would be very difficult to pay. Some people have lost their homes because the variable rate loan monthly payment increased to an amount that was impossible to pay.

Negative amortization is when the minimum monthly payment you are making in a variable rate program is not enough to cover the whole of the interest charge for that month. You can pay and pay on a $200,000 mortgage for 12 months only to discover at the end of the year that the unpaid balance of the mortgage is $202,000. This is not good. You should avoid getting into a situation where you have negative amortization on any loan you have. Negative amortization will cause erosion to your net worth.

With the variable rate loan, the interest rate is tied to a specific index. You need to know specifically what index your variable rate loan will be tied to. You need to be sure this index is fair and is not highly volatile. Highly volatile variable rate loan indexes cause the interest rate to soar with the slightest changes in the economy. Be sure you know the index and the maximum percentage of increase of your interest rate in any one year.

With the variable rate loan, you need to know the maximum interest charge that could possibly happen over the life of the loan. You need to know the minimum rate the lender will allow the loan to go to if the economy were to turn in your favor. Note that most all variable rate loans go up in interest rate faster than they are allowed to go down in interest rate. The rate will fluctuate with the index you are assigned. The index will fluctuate with the economy. There is a lot you need to know if you have a variable rate loan. Your bet in accepting the variable rate loan is that the interest rate for the life of the loan will be less than that of the fixed rate loan.

If you have a variable rate loan, be sure you plan to track the interest changes on the loan. This means that with the variable rate loan you have some homework to do. When your calculation and the lender's calculation do not agree, do not hesitate to call the lender and ask questions. Tell them your calculation and their calculation do not agree. Most borrowers think they are wrong and adjust their records to match the lenders.

Note that the variable rate loan and any loan that has negative amortization are tools that are used by experienced and expert real estate investors. These investors know exactly how to analyze all of the hidden costs and factors of the variable rate loan. They are always looking at the loan and to the property. They know from their experience how to make a profit in real estate by using these tools.

HOMEOWNER'S INSURANCE

When buying a house, mortgage insurance is often a topic for consideration. This is a form of life insurance that pays only the unpaid balance of your mortgage should something unexpected happen. Some lenders ask for this in case keeping up with your mortgage payments kills you unexpectedly!

There is better coverage out there for less money. Evaluate your insurance needs, making sure one of the life insurance policies you have will pay more than the outstanding balance of your home mortgage.

You will need to obtain a homeowner's policy. Sit with your insurance agent and be certain about what you are bargaining for. Ask if the policy has full replacement cost in the event of fire, storm, earthquake, flood or other hazard. Ask about what the policy does not cover. Shop the insurance rates and coverages with more than one agency. If you ask questions up front, you will reduce your surprises when you want the policy to pay. Inquire about the deductible portions of the policy. Compare the costs of higher deductible and lower deductible coverage.

Ask about duplication of coverage and what parts of the coverage could be eliminated because you are paying for something you will never need. Ask about what would qualify you for discounts on the various policies. Be certain you are getting sound, frank answers from the insurance agent before you buy. Inquire with other agents to see whether or not you are getting the best deal. If you have a friend in the insurance business that is in another line of insurance or will not be insulted that you are not buying coverage from them, ask them to review your policy before you sign. You may also want to inquire with an attorney who is skilled in home and auto insurance. Raise questions about full replacement cost coverage, earthquake insurance, flood insurance, storm damage claims, who pays them, what if the damage occurred over a long period of time and then finally gave way. These are important topics to discuss with your insurance agent and your attorney.

To assist your insurance company in the event of a claim, you will want to take still photographs and make videotapes of the entire house at least annually. Store these tapes in your safe deposit box or at someone else's house in a neighboring city. Likely this will be a relative. You can keep theirs and they can keep yours. In the event of fire or other hazard, you will find these off-site tapes and photos very valuable.

You may want your home and auto policy with the same insurance company. In doing this you may get extended coverage for many unanticipated events. You will get the "bundle" price. You can get an "umbrella" policy at very little cost that will cover you for liability that arises from personal acts, home accidents and auto accidents. This is very useful coverage at a very modest price.

SECOND MORTGAGES

In regard to the second mortgage on a house, there are a few factors to consider. Some lenders, after you have made prompt payments on your first mortgage for a while, will offer you a second mortgage, enticing you with money to spend on anything you want. Avoid temptation. Second mortgages erode the equity in your house and your net worth. The second mortgage can be like a stick of dynamite. You can take out the loan and play with it for a while. Then when you least expect it, the whole thing blows up in your hands. Most people cannot properly manage the money provided by a second mortgage. The bank is making the generous offer because you have worked hard to build equity in your home. Do not risk the loss of your home by spending money on things you do not need.

If you accept it and spend money to the maximum limit, you stand a chance of not being able to make the payments on the first or second mortgage. If this happens, then you lose your property. Avoid the second mortgage on your home.

There is one time that the second mortgage can be used as an effective tool to help you build net worth. This is when you accept the second mortgage to enable you to make a down payment on an investment rental property. This is a good way to get your real estate investment program going if you plan to purchase real estate investment properties. Once you have equity in the first home, use the second mortgage to make the down payment on the first investment property. Then when you have built more equity in your first home and you have equity in your investment property, use the equity of the two properties to purchase the next investment property. The art of going smaller to bigger has made multi-millionaires out of many people coast to coast.

SOME TAX POINTS YOU SHOULD KNOW

Tax basis is a tax law term referring to the value of your home: the cost of the home plus improvements, additional costs, and fees. This subtotal is then reduced by any depreciation you have claimed. The final tax basis, therefore, takes into consideration all of these adjustments.

It is important to keep track of the cost of purchasing your home and all other costs of improvement, refinancing, and other items that can be added onto the purchase cost of the home for tax purposes (i.e., that can increase the tax basis of the home.

The tax law requires that you keep your cancelled checks or check images and the invoice for the improvement or other cost of the property used to increase your basis. Two things cancelled check and an invoice. Some people own their home for 30 years. The tax law requires that you keep all 30 years of records, cancelled checks and invoices to support your claims for improvements that increase the tax basis in your home.

You must do some record keeping with each house you purchase. For starters, your purchase documents are lifetime records and should be kept with your permanent records throughout your life. After you purchase a house, the costs of refinancing or upgrading the house can be added to the costs of purchasing the home. You will need to keep careful track of the improvements you make to your home. It is advantageous for you to keep these records. The amount of profit you calculate when you sell your house will be less if you keep careful track of the costs you put into the house after you purchase it. Keep track of the cost and the related required documentation, the cancelled check and the invoice.

If you have more costs attributable to the house, you will have less profit on paper showing at the time of sale. As a result, you will pay ultimately less tax when your home is sold. For example, if you sell your house for $300,000 and have identified $200,000 in costs, you will have a tax profit of $100,000. If you sell your house for $300,000 and have identified $250,000 in costs, you will have a tax profit of $50,000. Less profit results in less tax due.

Under the current tax law you first calculate your tax profit resulting from the sale of your residence. You are under no obligation to find a new home. The first $250,000 of profit is forgiven for each adult that is party to the home ownership filing a single or joint return. Single people reduce their tax profit by $250,000. Married people reduce their tax profit by $250,000 each or $500,000.

More specifically, under the Internal Revenue Code, homeowners can potentially exclude up to $250,000 (or $500,000 for married couples filing jointly) in capital gains when selling their personal residence. To qualify, you must have owned and occupied the property as your primary residence for at least 24 out of the 60 months leading up to the close of escrow. This generous tax benefit is designed to help individuals and families reduce their tax liability when selling their homes, making it a valuable incentive for homeowners looking to move or downsize while preserving their hard-earned equity. Consult a tax professional for specific guidance.

There is movement afoot for Congress to change the numbers for certain states where houses cost more than the rest of the country. A similar measure is being considered regarding being able to deduct the full amount of mortgage interest and property taxes on one's personal residence.

Please note: you must maintain adequate records to prove the amount of additional costs you have incurred. You should have a large metal box that you keep somewhere. You should label this box with the address of your house.

Each time you incur costs in upgrading your house, you need to keep the cancelled checks in this box stapled to the invoices for the additional costs you have incurred.

This can be a very important set of records, especially if you keep your house for 20 years. Many people forget to keep these important records. When you purchase a home, it is important that you understand the necessity of keeping these records, especially the purchase closing statement and any refinancing of the property statements. You should set in place a record-keeping system that will help in tracking the improvement to the property costs over the years you own your home. You not only need to track the costs, but you must show the cancelled checks and the invoices showing the date and amount of costs involved.

If you know someone who has recently purchased a house, go out and buy them a good metal storage box and label the box with their address. Tell them how necessary it is to keep these records over the years of ownership of their new home. Help get them started in the right direction with their new investment.

This all sounds easy to do. I have seen many people misunderstand the rules and consequently they pay a tax they would not otherwise owe if they had sought the proper professional advice.

Note that we have discussed the tax events that take place when you sell real estate that is occupied by you as your personal residence. A completely different set of rules applies to real estate you hold as investment property. You are taxed differently on investment property. The main thing to know is that with investment real estate you cannot sell the property and pocket the funds. If you pocket the funds at all during any part of the transaction you will pay an income tax.

RETIREMENT PLANS

It is possible to save for retirement and build assets for retirement without having an actual retirement plan. I once had an interesting talk with a stockbroker. When I told him my client wanted to invest to meet his retirement goals, the stockbroker insisted this was almost illegal unless the client opened a corporate retirement plan.

There are several ways to fund for retirement. The tax laws do provide incentives for corporations, partnerships and sole proprietorships to start tax-qualified retirement plans for employers and employees. These are great. Realize, however, that you can make other plans in addition to these tax-qualified vehicles.

A note of caution to those of you who are receiving a lump sum from your employer at the end of your work stay with the company. You can roll that retirement plan into the next employer's plan without a tax consequence. You can also park the money in an IRA account until you find a new employer and not have to pay tax on those monies until you ultimately retire.

These are important and sophisticated tax moves that most tax preparers do not know and, thus, rarely pass on to their customers. If you are facing these decisions, you should be in the hands of a tax specialist, so you are properly informed before receiving your benefits. Thus, you can make the necessary tax moves before it is too late.

When you ultimately retire, big mistakes can be made. I have seen lawyers and accountants alike miss this planning step. If your employer offers you a chance to take the money in monthly payments or in one lump amount, take the lump amount and run.

The reason for this is that if you were to die two years after your retirement date and you elected to take the monthly payment method of retirement distribution, the employer's insurance company may keep any additional monies that had accumulated to your benefit with the exception that some plans pay a smaller monthly amount to your surviving spouse. If this were the case, when your wife dies (and legally she must be your wife), the money stops.

The 401(k) plans work differently because each year the money goes into your own personal account, held by a designated third party the employer designates. You will know who this is because they have to send you an annual summary and balance of your account.

If you take the lump sum, you can require yourself to invest the money and pledge to never touch the principal sums. The retirement money remains yours. The earnings from your investments should be comparable to the monthly amount the employer promised you. When you and your wife die, the money is there in your ownership and control to pass along to your children and grandchildren. The best place to put the lump sum is into your IRA account this way you control what you take out and then you will know how much you have to pay tax on. Note the IRS mandates that older people of a certain age take out minimum required distributions (RMD's). Be sure that you and your tax advisor are on top of this issue. Also, from time to time when you have years of being in lower tax brackets you can covert some of your IRA amounts into a Roth IRA account which may be to your advantage.

Here is an example. Say you have worked for a company and you have reached your retirement age. Then the company makes an offer to pay you the $500,000 of retirement benefits that have accumulated in your account. They then offer to pay you the $500,000 in one lump sum or in monthly payments of $400 per month for your lifetime and $200 per month for your wife if she were to survive you. In this case, if you take the monthly payments of $400 per month and then live two years after your retirement date, the company has paid you $400 x 24 months or $9,600. Basically, you have settled for $9,600 rather than the $500,000 you could have passed on to your wife or other heirs.

Selecting the appropriate retirement payoff can be quite tricky. Be sure you have competent advisors who are working for you and are not paid representatives of your employer.

In the case where you take the monthly payments, the principal sums are going to be kept by the employer. If you take the lump sum, you can forever have that money until you pass it along to your heirs. There is a tax on the lump sum distribution, but there are tax strategies that will allow you to roll over the money into an IRA account and not pay any tax on it until you actually withdraw the monies from the IRA account.

In almost all cases, it proves to be the wiser decision to take a lump sum from an employer. The time when this does not work is when the people are so irresponsible with money and the principal sums distributed by an employer are spent carelessly within a short period of time.

These irresponsible people could have become more responsible by reading this book. If you are not responsible enough to handle a big chunk of money, know yourself well enough to leave the money with the employer.

PENSION PLANS

Whether you are self-employed or are employed by a company, you will quite likely have the opportunity to participate in a pension plan. Pension plans have different names and labels, but they accomplish the same basic thing. They provide a tax-sheltered way to routinely put money aside for your retirement years. Like the IRA account, the pension plan can help you store up some cash for those retirement years. If you are self-employed, often there are many advantages that will allow quite a bit of cash to be sheltered inside the pension arrangement.

The advantage of pension arrangements is that the money funded each year is invested to generate interest, capital gain or dividends as earnings on the amounts funded. Those earnings are then added to the principal accumulations and the next year's funding. The whole ball keeps growing and growing tax free. The annual earnings on the investments are not taxed at the end of your tax year.

The disadvantage of the 401(k) style of pension plan is that the owner of the plan-you can raid the plan, take the principal and earnings out. If you do this you will pay income tax and a penalty if you are under age 59 ½. In the big picture this arrangement has not worked for the people very well because by the time you get to age 65 you have raided the account so many times that there is little there for retirement. Congress was pressured into letting the people invest their own money for retirement but overall, this method has failed many Americans.

With a regular personal savings account, each year you will fund the account. The savings are invested to generate interest, capital gain or dividend income. These earnings of dividends, capital gain or interest are taxed each year, reducing the amount that can go forward to next year. There is less to invest the following year under a regular savings plan than under a pension plan. This is due to the fact that the annual earnings are taxed yearly, reducing the money you have to invest the following year. Thus, if your savings account pays you 8% and you are in an income tax bracket of 30%, each year your 8% less taxes is an effective yield of 5.6% after the tax you pay. In a pension plan, you get to have the 8% earn and earn year after year without having to pay any tax annually.

Your regular savings account has tax erosion annually, reducing your after-tax yield on that investment. Money inside your pension plan is free of tax each year, so all of the yield you earn compounds and grows bigger and bigger each year.

Some employers offer their employees a pension arrangement where they will match the amount of funding placed in the plan by the employee. If you are the employee, take full advantage of all matching fund arrangements. The math on these arrangements computes great returns on your investment.

After you have stayed with your employer for the period of time described in your pension plan documents, then you become "vested" in your account with your employer. You are offered an incentive to stay with your employer. The longer you stay, the more you accumulate in your account, with full benefits going directly to you when you retire. Some people have quit work so they could get their hands on their pension money. This is very unwise and comes with severe tax consequences. Shifting employers to get your pension plan monies is not wise financial planning and only documents your short sighted and irresponsible ways of dealing with money.

For some pension plans the factors that go into determining how much is funded to your pension account each year is your base salary amount, your years of service with the company and your age until retirement.

When you terminate your service with an employer, you can put your pension monies into a special, separate IRA account until you have a new employer that will allow you to roll over your old retirement plan accumulations into their plan. You can have several new employers between the time the old employer gave you the pension distribution and the time a new employer agrees to let you roll over your money into their pension plan.

This is all a bit complex. In short, the pension tax due comes under a pay-me-now or pay-me-more-later decision. If you take the money now, you likely will be in a much higher tax bracket than you will be once you retire. When you are in a lower tax bracket, you can then begin withdrawing your IRA monies and get them into your possession by paying less tax than if you took the money when you were in the higher tax bracket.

Tax law requires you to begin withdrawing and paying tax on your IRA accumulations at age 73. This age amount will be changed by Congress from time to time. If you do not comply with these forced withdrawal requirements RMD's, severe penalties begin to accumulate that will put a great big dent in your IRA savings. You must begin a plan of withdrawal at age 73.

If you die and the IRA becomes part of your estate, your spouse has the rollover rights on the monies they receive and must begin withdrawing when they reach 73. Other beneficiaries will not have the same rollover rights and may be subject to tax under a set of complex rules for non-spouse beneficiaries.

Whether you have an IRA or an employer plan, you will have to sort out the money that went into either one that has already been taxed. You may have made voluntary contributions to the employer plan. You may have made nondeductible contributions to the IRA. In either case you will not be taxed again on the income that was taxed before it went into your plan.

From your diary records, you need to sort out the money that was already taxed and subtract it from the gross amount of the distribution to arrive at the amount subject to current taxation. You should have maintained good records in this regard by keeping a diary about each year. You should have permanent records for your pension and IRA investments in which you log in your annual contributions. Then make note of whether these contributions we already subject to tax or were these voluntary nondeductible amounts, you need to know these numbers, year by year so you don't get taxed twice. With this list you will be able to retrieve the necessary information to determine what is currently subject to federal tax and what is subject to state tax.

One more thing check with you tax advisor once all the money is settled in your IRA account then investigate whether you are eligible to use the tax brackets and make decisions of putting a little of the IRA money each year into a Roth account.

TAX-SHELTERED SAVINGS ACCOUNTS

IRA accounts, which are allowed as tax-sheltered savings account under the Unites States tax system, are the best way for individuals to commence saving money for their retirement years. Until the drafters of the tax laws see what great strength would come to the United States if individuals were given the incentive to save more money, the annual maximum contribution is a very modest sum. As more understanding is gained on what great strength would come from greater savings, the annual contribution should be increased. You cannot count on your IRA to provide enough money to carry you through your retirement years. It is a good supplement to your other retirement investment strategies.

Through an IRA alone there is not an individual in the United States that would not have $300,000 in retirement savings if they funded the IRA each year of their work career. If the household has two career workers, then there could be $600,000. Everyone can do this, but it takes discipline. That's all it takes. With $300,000 in retirement savings, at the yield of 10% each year, you could have $30,000 in retirement investment earnings to cover your annual expenses. Keep in mind that this is just from your IRA savings. If you fund the maximum amount each year and continue to do so year after year, the money begins to accumulate in a very rapid way and a nice sum is available to you at age 65. The key to a successful IRA is to fund each year. rain or shine, keep funding.

In certain instances, you may not be eligible for a deduction for paying into your IRA account. If this occurs, you can still fund the IRA account, and you should. If you fund your nondeductible IRA amounts, this can generate investment earnings that will not be taxed until many years down the road. You can build on savings and earnings year after year without any of the investment earnings being taxed.

Your IRA account comes with some record keeping requirements. You should maintain an investment book in which you log in the amount you have funded your IRA account each year. You should note how much of what you funded that year was a federal deduction and how much of it was a state deduction. These records will be very important many years down the line when you are retired and commence withdrawing from your IRA account. If you know the amount of funding and the amount of deduction allowed, you will not be taxed twice on the same money, a risk you could run if you do not keep track of this important information every year you fund your IRA account.

LIFE INSURANCE

If you have life insurance, you should have your insurance owned by a life insurance trust. If you invested diligently and your net worth is over a million dollars, the life insurance trust keeps the life insurance from becoming taxed in your estate.

Life insurance is a kind of investment. It is a special kind of investment. With life insurance, you set money aside in a kind of savings account. If you live to a ripe old age, this will not be your best investment. If you die at an early age, this investment will make you look like the smartest person on earth. Life insurance is designed to be there in case you die young. Life insurance provides for the unknown and the unexpected. Life insurance helps your family and loved ones once you are not here by providing for them. If the life insurance company is called upon to pay off early, you will have invested very little and they will pay your loved ones a lot of money. Check with your friendly life insurance agent and find out what type and style of life insurance is best for your overall financial picture.

PURCHASING AN AUTOMOBILE

You need to develop a sound strategy for purchasing an automobile. Before buying an automobile, you need to do some research. Yes, this means you have to read. Go to your local library. Go on the internet. Look through performance magazines. Observe the performance and horsepower ratings offered. Read about how your target car compares to other cars in its class. Then get to the consumer information magazines. Locate the invoice price for the car. Yes, the dealer invoice price is published in a number of free publications at your local library and on the internet. Go to the dealership equipped with this information. If you are a member of AAA (American Automobile Association), part of the service they offer is to research for you the dealer invoice price and dealer cost of any car you want to buy. You need to enroll and become a member before you can use this service. The annual fee is not high, and the fee also allows you and family members to have use of their emergency roadside service. Call AAA in your area and ask about the services they have to offer.

Call a car dealership before you go in; ask to speak directly to the owner. It may save you a commission in the deal if you come into the transaction through the owner of the business. The owner may also elect to refer you to a salesperson. Test-drive the car. Make sure it is going to meet your needs. Make the best deal with the salesperson. Many dealers will show you the invoice price. This may be misleading because there are discounts, incentives and bonuses the dealer makes even if you buy the car at the published or listed invoice price.

One thing is for sure, there is a lot going on behind the scenes when you are in the dealership. It might be good to be ready to purchase right at the end of a calendar quarter. Many dealerships have targets they want to reach. Your purchase may win them a trip or gain some other benefit for the dealership. The end of the quarter is a good time to make a deal. Also, you can buy a new car at the end of the model year. If a dealer still has some new cars that are last year's model, you may find you get a new car at a very affordable price. Shop right, buy right. Do your homework and research before you set foot on a car dealer's premises.

Whether to buy or lease the car is strictly an economic decision. The old rule of thumb was that if you were going to turn the car in every two years and get another one, you should lease. If you were going to keep the car for more than three years, you should buy.

You need to make a list, with one page titled "Buy" and one page titled "Lease."

If you buy the car, consider the down payment, the monthly payments of principal and interest and the equity buildup you might have after 60 months.

Compare this to the lease: the down payment, the excess mileage charges and the cost to purchase the vehicle at the end of the lease period.

Leases are always constructed to tease you into taking them. In the past they were tricky ways to get you to pay 20% or more interest on the money spent on the car. Leases always allow you to drive the car for less per month than if you were to get a bank loan and make monthly payments. Leases become economically unwise when you get to the end of the lease period. You have no equity. You may have to pay something to get out of the lease. You might have to pay an excess mileage charge. If you want to purchase the car at the end of the lease, the big payment will propel you past the sum of the payments you would have made had you bought the car in the beginning.

Your decision to lease or buy should be made based on the economics of the transaction. Evaluate which program will cost you less money once you have considered all of the factors in the big picture. Just because the lease is less per month does not make it the better economic choice for you.

If you have a choice, have the car owned by a corporation. Corporate ownership of a vehicle combined with your insurance could significantly limit your exposure to liability if you are involved in an auto accident.

If you personally own your automobiles, be sure you are adequately insured. Ask your insurance person about an umbrella policy that will come into play if you were to exceed the limits of coverage on your automobile policy. You want to be sure to have adequate coverage so your assets are protected from an unforeseen legal judgment.

COLLEGE EDUCATION

If you have children, you need to consider very early on in their life what your plans are for their college education.

You need to consider if you are going to pay for your child's college education. Is your child expected to pay? Are you going to share the cost with your child? Are you going to pay and then ask your child to repay you once they are working? Are you going to sponsor your child into the working world by providing them with the necessary tools to obtain good employment?

These are major questions that need to be asked and answered. You need to talk these matters over with your spouse so you both have the same idea as to how college education will be handled financially.

The earlier you can commence saving and earning toward college, the better off you will be. Do not wait until your child reaches age 18 and then raid your only savings as you struggle to pay the high cost of college education.

College education has many known and unknown costs. On the surface are the costs of room, food, tuition, books and spending money. Other costs are health insurance, medical costs, transportation costs, special program costs, travel expenses and other unforeseen costs. The range of costs can be between $25,000 and $200,000 for each of your children for a four-year degree at a college that is not even one of the top schools in the country.

If you have three children, you need to get ready for this substantial cash outlay. Where is it going to come from? One thing for sure is that it is not going to come raining out of the clouds when your child reaches age 18.

The children who benefit least from college planning are those children whose parents are divorced. It is difficult to collect and pay child support up to age 18. Each year support is paid and each year support is spent. Neither spouse gives much thought to college savings. Many times, there is an ongoing feud that stems from the divorce itself. The feud limits the willingness to openly communicate about the college needs of the child.

To help your child, stop the feud. Open a savings account or brokerage account with your favorite brokerage firm. Set up the account or irrevocable trust in the name of the child and earmark that account for college savings. Require that both spouses be signers on the account or appoint a neutral third party to act as trustee, someone who will be unbiased toward the feuding spouses and will act in the best interests of the child. If the spouses have incomes that are drastically different, out of caution you should get together with a lawyer seasoned and experienced in family law matters. Require that this account be used only for college education, and in no way limit or reduce the annual contribution of each spouse for the support of the child.

In the event the child does not go to college before reaching age 25, you can set out in your agreement how the monies will be disbursed. If college is not attended, give all the money to the child but spread it out over a 15-year period. You could pay out the fund by giving one-third to the child, one-third to the father and one-third to mother, or you could base the payout for reimbursement upon the financial amounts contributed by the father and the financial amounts contributed by the mother.

This format has proven to be very helpful in getting children of divorced couples funded for a college education.

Another important matter in dealing with college education is to require your child to go to the placement office of the college they are enrolled in. This trip should occur within the first six months of attending college. Have them become aware of the job opportunities for graduating seniors in their field of study. Have them list where these jobs are located, the amount of compensation at the start of the job, and the amount of compensation at the peak of that career. Within the first year of college, they should visit with someone who is actually employed in their field of study. Have the child make inquiries about the compensation, lifestyle, hours and working conditions. Ask these people about the amount of time they have off to enjoy their families and to participate in healthy recreation.

By having your child conduct such studies and fieldwork as a requirement of further college funding, you will limit your chances of spending your hard-earned money on a college education that leads to no real job at the end. Many history majors have been shocked after four or five years of college training to see that there was not an appealing job waiting for them on graduation day. This is all part of the parents' college education management.

Among the classes your children take, you might want to suggest some courses in computer science and business administration. This is primarily because the computer is part of every household as well as part of every work site. Your child will be entering the business world soon after graduation, and they, too, are going to have to become good investment managers. This is a certainty. If they are going to enter the business world, you would think they would want to take some business courses.

Most colleges have career counseling offices that will help your child match their individual skills with an appropriate major. Many career counseling offices conduct or know of testing that will help identify which occupations your child is best suited for. This is valuable information and should be sought out by every college attendee. Some children are more creative and would do better in architecture. Some children are more oriented toward details and would do better in accounting or engineering. A sad example of what can happen is the child of an accountant pursuing an accounting education. They struggle all the way, enter the business world and find out all those details are not for them. They might be better suited for jobs that require or utilize more creativity. It is better for everyone that the proper career match be made at an early age. The testing and information is available. Most college career counseling offices have a variety of tests that can determine which occupations best suit someone's personality.

It is hard for parents to direct their children. At college age you want them to be making their own decisions, and they also prefer it that way. After all, it is their future. You should be available if they seek your help or advice. Have an open-door policy and encourage the child to seek your advice.

You can see that college planning requires much more than just saving for college. College planning requires sound management and decision-making skills on the part of you and your child.

Other complications can occur. What if your child does well in college and wants to go to graduate school or medical school? How are you going to financially handle this? You need to set the policy in advance, and you also need to be flexible enough to help a truly talented child.

One last note about how to help your child in regard to their retirement future. Often overlooked is the power of investing and then the compounding of the investment yield on the original investment year after year. If you want to assist your children toward their retirement plans, you can adopt the following money management strategy. Invest $2,000 per year for your child from the time the child is age 14 until the child is age 20. Then stop funding. Leave the money alone and try to achieve 10% or greater return on this investment. You will surprise your child. When they reach age 65, they will have over $100,000 available to them. Try to do this for each child.

SOCIAL SECURITY

Social Security is designed to provide a monetary benefit from the federal government when workers retire or become disabled. The amounts are paid directly to the workers or to their families. The Social Security Act enacted by Congress in 1935 set up the initial framework for the Social Security system as we know it today.

Today people in the work force between the ages of 25 and 65 contribute to the Social Security system. These funds are paid to people who are eligible and over the age of 62. As long as there are more workers in the work force than there are receivers of the money in the retirement force, the system should survive, although the system is in great need of overhaul and adjustment.

Social Security comes from payroll taxes paid half by the employee and half by the employer. Your money, when withheld, is not invested by the government and held for you in your account with your name on it. Instead, the Social Security system works like a "Ponzi scheme" in which the last person in pays for the person who invested long ago and is now retired. The 25 year old entering the work force is paying the 65 year old who retires. We have seen the effect of swells to the population. What will happen when the number in the work force is less than the number in the retirement population? Needless to say, the system needs to be overhauled and the retirement sums need to be increased.

The basic provisions of the Social Security program allow for a guaranteed monthly income designed to ensure a basic level of financial support for retired or disabled people, their families and their survivors. It is funded by money that is withheld from your paycheck and then matched with your employer's contribution.

You are eligible for federal Social Security benefits if you have legally worked in the United States and have contributed to the fund. The Social Security Administration keeps records of the number of calendar quarters you have worked. These are tallied up to determine the Social Security benefits you are eligible for. The amount of eligibility is based upon your earned income and the number of calendar quarters you have worked. You may at any time contact the Social Security

Administration and ask them to tell you about the number of quarters of credit you have.

I recommend to my clients that after they have reached the age of 50, they contact Social Security every five years and get a copy of the report that tells them the credit they have been given and the amount of benefits they have become eligible for.

Basically, you feed the Social Security system each year you work. Your income is then indexed so there are comparable numbers to work with. Your basic benefit is computed based on your earnings over 40 quarters. This amount becomes somewhat permanent. Then, as Congress allows, there is an annual cost of living adjustment made to your monthly benefit. Your benefit is then based upon your base rate plus cost-of-living adjustments and determined by the age you are at the time of first receiving your benefits.

You may start collecting Social Security monthly benefits once you reach age 62. If you expect to live a long time, it is better to wait until age 65 to begin collecting benefits. I have seen people contemplate this decision for months. If you begin receiving benefits at age 63, you get less. If you live long enough, you get more money for waiting until age 65 to collect monthly benefits. The earlier you begin, the less your monthly benefit will be. It's time for you to get out a pad of paper and pencil so you can make the computations to compare what is better for you. Although the benefit is less at age 62, you may need to live to more than 75 to become penalized for taking the lesser amount. The present trend is for Social Security to adjust the retirement age to an age over 65. This means in years after 1995 you will have to be over the age of 65 to receive benefits. Soon you may have to be age 70 to receive benefits under the system. Your year of birth and the changes in the law determine at what age you will become eligible for your Social Security benefits.

Your spouse is entitled to Social Security benefits. Upon reaching age 62, they are entitled to some benefit, and then at age 65 they will be entitled to roughly half of your monthly benefit. Your spouse may be entitled to full benefits if they worked the 40 quarters required by Social Security. Divorced spouses may be entitled to some of your benefits. What a shocking thought! They may become eligible to receive benefits after turning age 62. Their benefits will be determined based upon your earnings, provided they were married to you for at least 10 years and have not remarried. If a divorced spouse remarries, this benefit stops. Then they become eligible when their new spouse starts receiving Social Security benefits. If you become eligible for benefits and your divorced spouse is raising a child that is under 16, then they are eligible for a benefit that is equal to one-half of the benefit you are receiving. You will always receive your full benefit. The benefit a spouse draws does not reduce the amount you actually receive. They are always given an additional benefit from the Social Security system. If you retire and still have children under age 18, they may become eligible for Social Security benefits.

Once you reach retirement age you are given the benefits for which you are eligible. If you have done well and your individual taxable income is high, you must report your Social Security entitlement on your income tax return. The government taxes you on your Social Security earnings as a means to get back some of what they have paid you. Rather than go back into the Social Security fund, the amount is collected as income tax. It then goes into the general fund to be spent by the government for their various programs. Thus, you keep only a portion of the Social Security benefits you are given.

If you contacted Social Security and received a copy of your printed summary, you may take it to a Social Security office near you. A benefits counselor can then sit with you and at no charge tell you what benefits you qualify for. You should make an appointment with a benefits counselor to eliminate or greatly reduce your wait time in their office.

MANTRA

I will start my investment accounts and program at a very early age and build these investments into a strong financial future for myself and my family.

CHAPTER 11

The Retirement Years

People often think about their retirement years. Periodically they day-dream about or actively visualize these years. Few people, however, take the time to financially plan for their retirement. In counseling people who are concerned about and aware of their desire to have prosperity in their retirement years, I link all of this together. I connect their dreams up with their financial capability of reaching those dreams. I chart the course the clients must take. My staff consultants prepare spreadsheets and computerized financial models of what their retirement years will look like. We show them where their income will come from, in what quantities and at what frequency. Financial security is a desire most people share. Retirees especially want to be able to maintain a comfortable lifestyle.

With the current trends in population shift, increasing consumer costs, rising health care costs, shifts in corporate pension arrangements and government spending cutbacks, you need to give some thought early in your life toward saving for the retirement years. It is obvious that you will have to be the source of your retirement income. Planning for a secure financial future is something you must do for yourself. If you include your spouse, you can support each other's efforts toward funding your retirement nest egg.

When you become older and you are considering retirement, you reflect back on your opportunities and ability to build wealth, preserve your wealth and protect your wealth. Your activities during retirement are going to be limited if you have not properly planned and saved for the retirement years. In considering retirement, you need to consider when you will retire and what your needs and resources will be in retirement. Then you need to compare your resources to your needs.

Some additional issues need to be raised. You need to consider; what city you will live in when you retire, what your housing cost is going to be, and what activities, social events, clubs and organizations you will belong to. What friendships will you cultivate and what steps will you take to meet new people? You also need to consider family contacts, recreation, sports, exercise and your emotional and spiritual needs. The main objective seems to be a comfortable life. You need to consider how well you are going to adjust to living on a fixed income. Your satisfaction with retirement will come with how adequately your financial resources meet your needs.

We provide retirement counseling for those who do not feel comfortable about or ready for complete retirement. Some have fears of what a fixed income will do to them. Some have worries that inflation will erode their financial abilities during retirement. These are very real worries. We work with our clients to find solutions. This adds comfort, structure and stability to their retirement plans. For many people, retirement requires transition to a new lifestyle. Some people struggle with this and feel abandoned by their company. Some people get very depressed when they consider retirement. For most people, however, it is like taking a duck to water; they jump right in and enjoy those golden years of life.

Currently, about one million people a year are retiring between the ages of 60 and 65. The population is changing. Presently one in every five Americans is over the age of 65.. With modern medical practices and a diet-conscious generation, the average life expectancy could be well in excess of age 85. Thus, your retirement life could span more than 20 years. You need to take the proper planning steps and be financially positioned to retire and stay retired for this 20-year period.

I want to emphasize that there is no requirement of working to age 65, folks! If you have some ingenuity and motivation and catch the right opportunity wave, you can retire at 40 or younger. You have to work smart, not hard. Definitely you do not have to "put in your time." You do, however, need to amass the financial wherewithal to fully and financially retire.

After you begin building net worth and amassing financial strength, work becomes a "want to" and is not a "have to." Retirement is whatever you want it to be. It does not mean that you stay home and watch game shows on TV. Retirement can include starting a new business enterprise, or it may include endless days on the golf course, on a sailboat, in your garden or a combination of all these pursuits.

Part of your financial game plan should be to retire in style. Having taught many courses on net worth building and retirement planning, I find that retiring in style is the mission of each person I have had the opportunity to guide and counsel.

With retirement comes financial responsibility. Every individual needs to know well in advance of their retirement date that they are going to be called upon in their retirement years to be their own financial manager. Each one of us is going to be a financial manager in the future. Should this not tell us to get as much training along the way in this subject as we can tolerate and absorb? If you carefully look at each retiree, you will see that their income stems from interest, dividends, rents, family business, pensions and other sources.

You are entitled to Social Security. You will have funds available through your company's pension plan and your individual retirement account savings. Then you have those assets you have accumulated with your career earnings. If you were a good student of this book you would own 18 rental units that pay rents that keep pace with inflation.

To compare your efficiency in converting career earnings into investments, it is always interesting to compute your career earnings. Try it. Add up all of your annual earnings for the past 40 years. Put as the numerator the present-day net value of your accumulated assets, not counting your IRA savings. Put as the denominator the sum of your career earnings. What percentage do you calculate? This is how you measure the efficiency of converting your career earnings into retirement-minded investments.

While writing this book, I asked retirees what they would tell the younger generation. The message is the same from all of the people I spoke with: Tell the younger generation to save a portion of their earnings each year, beginning at age 25. Then increase that savings amount as your career earnings increase. Remember that $2,000 per year starting at age 25 will make available to you $500,000 in cash when you reach age 65. If you and your spouse do that one step, then you will have a combined amount of $1,000,000 for your retirement years. The $1,000,000 may provide you with $100,000 per year to spend as you please. Thus, you will have accomplished your objective to retire in style from only this one investment step.

In order to produce the amount of income you will want for you and your family in the retirement years, you will need to position your money in such a way that you earn the highest possible return on your investments. This sets forth the need for you personally to be your own investment manager. You and your spouse are going to be the investment managers for your family assets. It is better to become comfortable with this idea at an early age.

Investment training, reading and know-how are necessary to maximize your retirement income. You will need to know what you want to invest in and for how long. The total of your assets when you reach retirement age becomes the principal sums you have to invest. It is important to understand the distinction between the principal sums you have to invest and the other part, which is the earnings from investing your principal sums. When you invest in your retirement years, you must invest without subjecting the principal you have accumulated to very much risk of loss.

During your lifetime you have generated income. You have saved, invested and converted that income into accumulations that you normally liquidate at your retirement date. You do this by scaling back and selling some of your assets so you have some cash for retirement. The total of your financial assets are your principal accumulations. These principal accumulations, when invested, create earnings or investment income. Let me provide an illustration. You have financial resources that are able to be separated into two baskets. The first basket is the principal basket. In my consulting practice and in my office, we call this the "rock." The second basket is the investment earnings basket. Normally, you do your spending during your retirement years from the basket of investment earnings.

If you invest the principal basket in such a way that your investment earnings are high, then you will have more spending money. You want to preserve the principal basket, your financial rock. Each year you want to measure the size of the rock and assure yourself that it has not become smaller. If the rock shrinks, you will have fewer resources to invest. Consequently, your investment income will shrink. When your investment income shrinks, your spending will have to decrease.

If you are a good investment manager, you must each year measure the size of your rock with increasing frequency. You do not want to have any shrinkage. When shrinkage occurs, you are eroding the amount of principal you can invest. As a consequence, the amount of your annual spendable income will go down.

Stated another way, if you keep your principal sums intact, they should not become less due to market changes, bad investments or over-spending on personal needs. Then you will be able to generate more annual income for spending from the principal sums invested. This simple principle is often incomprehensible to retirees. An example is if you have $500,000 that generates $50,000 per year of investment earnings. This gives you $50,000 for personal spending. If you spend too much and end up with $400,000 of principal to invest, you will have in this example only $40,000 for personal spending each year.

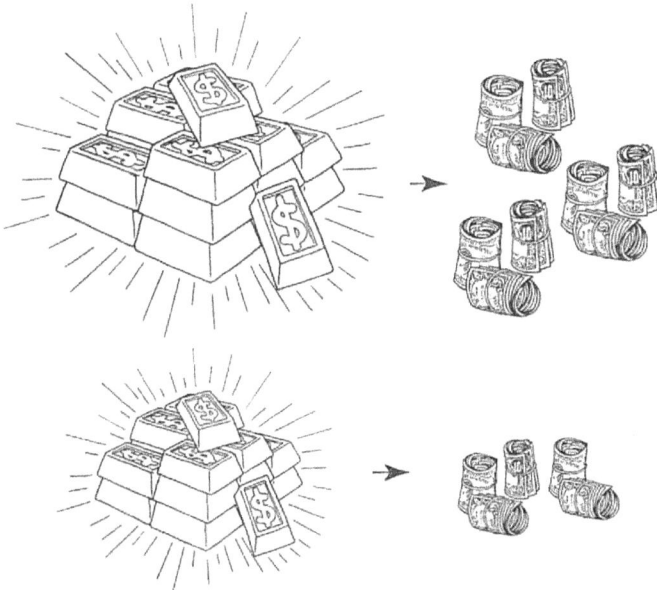

Your "rock" or principal investments will yield annual income for your retirement years. If you deplete the principal sums you invest, the income available to you will be significantly reduced.

If you maintain your principal accumulations and each year invest them to generate a return of 10%, then you will have money generated in your investment income basket. Another example would be when you have one million dollars invested at 10%. This yields investment income of $100,000 each year. If you do this every year, then your investment earnings basket has $100,000 available to spend each year. Each year you will have generated another $100,000, and retirement life goes on in fine style.

If you invade the principal sums and start spending your principal accumulations, then you will end up in financial trouble. If you invest in such a way that the market or bad investments eat up your principal sums, you will also end up in financial trouble.

Another example of this is based on the above instance where you have one million dollars in principal sums at the beginning of your retirement years that yield 10% or $100,000 of annual investment earnings. If you invade or lose some of your principal and you end up with $700,000 in principal sums at 10%, your annual investment income will only be $70,000. If you lose more and then have principal sums of $500,000, you will only have $50,000 of investment earnings annually. You can see how your annual available income decreases from $100,000 to $50,000. As the erosion of the rock continues, you get yourself to the point of not having enough annual income to meet your financial needs. When you run out of money, your only hope is that your kids really like you and will help out with your living expenses. For most parents, this is not a realistic financial plan.

If you start your retirement years with principal sums of less than one million dollars, then the numbers work the same. For example, if you start your retirement years with principal sums of $300,000 and your yield is 10%, then your annual income will be $30,000. If your principal sums erode away to $150,000, your annual income at 10% yield will be $15,000.

You can see that your earnings from investments are like your retirement salary. You get an annual salary from the principal sums invested in the form of your investment earnings. Your investment earnings are your salary. You can decide to save a portion of your salary and increase your principal sums, or you can decide to spend your salary on your personal needs.

Spending depletes your financial resources.

In retirement, one needs to live from the investment earnings only. The principal accumulations must be preserved as the tool to generate more retirement income.

When you retire, you have a sum total of assets that should be mathematically expressed as "principal sums accumulated." These principal accumulations are like a giant rock. The Rock of Gibraltar was used in many insurance advertisements. If you want the security of knowing your retirement will be rock solid, you need to heed this advice. Do not invade the principal accumulations.

Principal accumulations may start being collected when you are very young. The windfalls of bonuses, sales, inheritances and other happenings in life should be rolled up in a ball and added to one another to make one giant ball of principal for your retirement years. This concept is best illustrated by considering a snowball. You start with a very small ball, maybe the size of a marble, then hand-pack it until you have a tennis ball, then a basketball. Then you put it on the ground and roll it in more snow to make one giant snowball.

This is the same with principal accumulations. Your mission with your finances is to make one giant snowball that you can have and enjoy in your retirement years.

Upon retirement, you measure the size of the snowball and then you fight your hardest to maintain the exact same size income. Your spending is done from the income. The amount of spending has to be less than the size of your income to keep from invading principal and thus shrinking the snowball.

Note that many states require you to give away your snowball if your health deteriorates to such a degree that you need government assistance. Professional attorneys and accountants who are aware of the needs involved in elder care can help you and your estate planner properly position your assets in this regard. A helpful book on this subject is *How to Protect Your Life Savings from Catastrophic Illness and Nursing Homes*, by Harley Gordon.

Once you have lost your snowball or the rock referred to earlier, then back to work you go. Therefore, do not run from the fright of the words "investment management." Regardless of how much you accumulate for your retirement years, you, too, will become an investment manager, managing your own account. You and your spouse are going to be the investment managers for your family's assets. It is better to become comfortable with this idea at an early age.

You can break through these fears by training yourself. This includes taking courses and reading books and newspapers on investments. Like golf, tennis or bike riding, it is a skill that is learned, and when you practice over and over again, you improve your skill. Everyone is capable of learning how to manage their own investments.

No one in the world is going to take better care of your investments than you are.

When you retire, you should consider joining the American Association of Retired Persons (AARP), which passes along many good financial planning ideas to seniors. They have available numerous articles and publications that could be quite helpful to you. It might be wise for younger people to know about these ideas, too. AARP is very well respected and one of the strongest lobbying organizations working with Congress for the benefit of retired persons.

AARP has a membership of over 40 million people. They offer a wide range of programs and services for people over the age of 50. They can be contacted thru the internet, then have chat, and thru social media you can make contact with AARP.

AARP, American Association of Retired Persons
601 E Street NW
Washington, DC 20049
800-424-3410

Seniors are entitled to a number of discounts on almost everything they do. You need to be observant of senior discounts and at what age you will be eligible for senior discount on the goods and services you purchase.

Additionally, once you reach age 65 you are entitled to Medicare. Medicare was enacted by Congress in 1965 by way of the Medicare Act. Its purpose was to provide for the health care needs of older people. Medicare was not designed to cover all of the costs of elder health care. It was designed to defray the cost. Some of the cost was designed to be borne by the participants by way of premiums paid, deductible amounts paid, coinsurance and charges in excess of allowable charges. You can purchase supplemental insurance to pay for some of the charges that Medicare does not cover. You can also purchase insurance for covering long-term health care. This would pay for nursing home care if you were ever to be so confined. By having the coverage, you do not have to give away all of your assets to become eligible for state and federal assistance programs.

You can consider living in continuing care retirement communities. These are communities to which you pay an entry fee or sign an agreement and in turn they agree to provide for your lifetime care, whatever it may require. They are retirement communities that have a full line of activities and social programs for you to participate in.

Some income tax considerations of retirement have to do with the place you choose to retire. Certain states do not have an income tax. This has been a consideration of many retirees. The states of Alaska, Florida, Nevada, New Hampshire, South Dakota, Tennessee, Texas, Washington and Wyoming presently do not have an income tax.

Some of the financial factors you must consider in order to remain retired are:

activities	housing
autos	insurance
children	medical supplies
clothing	professional services
dental care	recreation
entertainment	relatives
exercise	repairs
eye care	social clubs
food	social gatherings
furnishings	supplies
gifts	taxes
grandchildren	travel
health care	utilities
household items	entertaining friends

Get a clear picture in your mind. Visualize what you want to do in your retirement years and begin moving in that direction now. As in business, you need to form your business plan to get to where you want to be in your retirement years.

The main principle to remember is that there is no law that states you must work to age 65, then retire.

Gain a clear vision of the amount and sources of your abundance.

Begin investing at an early age. The more you save over a long period of time, the more you will accumulate and have available in your retirement years.

Most people act like sheep during their career. They work hourly jobs, sometimes without expending a lot of thought or effort. Then they grow old and retire.

When you take charge of your life and step forward courageously and create wealth, you can retire when you have captured satisfactory financial resources.

The world is your oyster. You are unsupervised and left in charge of finding the way, the motivation, the desire, the energy and the opportunity to pry it open.

Motivated people have retired in style in their forties, never having to work another day in their lives.

Now that we have discussed and seared into your mind that retirement can happen at any age, know that retirement usually follows your career. Your work years should be a substantial coordinated effort to do something to generate earnings. Then you convert those earnings into investments. With these investment accumulations you are set to retire.

You conduct this substantial coordinated effort when you become motivated to do so. You become motivated to put forth this effort once you have become absolutely sure that only you hold the reins to control your financial destiny. Once you stand on your own two feet and take charge of your destiny, good things begin to happen.

You must create retirement principal sums by exerting your own personal effort with a large degree of enthusiasm and intensity.

Surround yourself with positive stimuli: books, tapes, videos and seminars. Learn to know you are in charge of your own financial future. Know that you are working hard to help yourself, your spouse and your family.

During your career, once you have overcome all of what are usually self-created roadblocks—your fears and endless excuses for being unsuccessful—then you will learn that you really can earn substantial profits to carry you into a prosperous future.

You are in charge of the health and well-being of your financial future. Take the steps today that will enable you to retire in style.

MANTRA

I will do whatever is necessary to retire in style with my spouse by my side.

Daily Affirmations

Use this list to create the positive inputs you need for success. These work best when you read them, then speak them out loud. They work especially well when you read them to each other in bed.

I am the source of my financial abundance.

I love and trust my imagination.

My thoughts are loving and positive toward others.

My choices and possibilities are expanding every day.

I am an unlimited human being.

I can create anything I want.

I picture abundance for myself and others.

My dreams come true.

I live in an abundant universe.

I radiate self-esteem, inner peace, love, well-being and happiness.

I create money and abundance through joy, aliveness and self-love.

Everything I do brings me aliveness and growth.

I know the essence of what I want and I get it.

Everything I create fulfills me.

The things I create are even better than I imagined them to be.

My energy is focused and directed toward my goals of money management.

I am increasingly magnetic to money, prosperity and abundance.

I create what I want with energy and my dynamic nature.

Good things come to me easily.

I am a champion net worth builder.

I trust and follow my inner guidance.

I spend quiet reflective time; I hear my inner guidance.

I am always in the right place at the right time.

I always follow my highest joy of building financial freedom.

I honor myself in everything I do.

I always choose the path of most light.

I honor my integrity in all that I do.

I am success.

I allow myself to feel financially successful.

I congratulate myself for my financial success.

I forgive myself, knowing that I did the best I knew how at the time.

I learn from my past mistakes.

I love getting there as much as being there.

I will manage my newfound wealth carefully.

I will enjoy and savor the space of doing well and continue in that spot-light for as long as I can.

My beliefs create my reality.

I believe in unlimited prosperity.

I am worthy of abundance and prosperity.

I invite abundance and prosperity into my life.

I feel the warmth of abundance relieving my stress.

I feel the warmth of prosperity lifting my burden.

I have a willingness and a desire to learn new things.

I am getting better and better in every way.

I choose beliefs that bring me aliveness and growth.

I enjoy learning new things.

I am proud of what I do and I am building for the future.

I will take those actions that will move me closer to what I want.

My beliefs create good things for me.

I deserve abundance.

I forgive my parents and wish them well.

Money flows into my life.

I am prosperous.

My energy is open and flowing in every area of my life.

I always have more money coming in than going out.

I search out new investments carefully.

I allow myself to have more than I ever dreamed possible.

I eliminate consumer debt from my life every day.

My value and my worth are increased by everything I do.

All my experiences are opportunities to gain more power, clarity and vision.

I send love to my fears.

My fears are the place within me that awaits my love.

I work each day to overcome my fears.

I monitor my fears and evaluate if they ever come to pass.

I have unlimited positive power and energy. I have overcome my fears in life.

I speak of success and prosperity, my words uplift and inspire others.

I live in an abundant world, I compete to get my share.

My world is safe, abundant and friendly.

I expect only the best to happen and it does.

I trust my ever-increasing ability to create abundance.

I accept prosperity and abundance in my life.

I trust that everything comes at the perfect time in the perfect way.

I demonstrate love with my actions every day.

I am linked with the unlimited abundance of my world.

As I do what I love, money and abundance flow freely to me.

I have a unique special contribution to make to the world.

I have used the gifts that I have been given with intensity.

Everything I do adds beauty, light, harmony and order to my world.

My wealth grows and multiplies daily.

I am successful and abundant in all areas of my life.

I reach my investment goals with excitement and ease.

I joyously provide for my retirement.

I want to retire in style at age 55.

Do what you love and the money will come.

I honor and use my special skills and abilities.

I have a wealth of valuable gifts, skills and talents.

I am working toward the vision of my ideal life.

I know what I love to do and I do it.

I allow myself to think and dream in unlimited ways.

All the answers are within me; I follow my inner wisdom.

I am a valuable person; my path is important.

My path and my life's work are my highest priorities.

I accept and love myself for who I am right now.

I honor and value my creativity.

I am a special and unique person.

I have ambitions of building high financial net worth.

My days are filled with fun and meaningful activities.

I give myself permission to be all that I can be.

I commit to my path. I choose aliveness and growth.

I follow my heart.

I can have what I want.

I invite and allow good to come into my life.

I flow with the current. I know that everything happens for my higher good.

I am alert to my opportunities and I use them well.

I release anything that is not for my higher good and ask it to release me.

I love and honor everything that I create.

I share my wealth and happiness with others in a careful loving way.

I let go easily, trusting that nothing leaves my life unless something better is coming.

I change the world around me by changing myself.

I bring love and a positive attitude to everything I do.

I create what I want easily and effortlessly.

I am a magnet to my higher good and it is a magnet to me.

I am abundantly provided for as I follow my path.

I know my value and I honor my worth.

People honor and value my work.

I always give my best.

I am productive with what I do every day in every way.

My time management skills are honed.

All of my spending is done in a careful way, using techniques to build my net worth.

I surround myself with things that reflect my aliveness and positive energy.

I appreciate all that I am and all that I have created.

I appreciate my spouse and all that I am and all that I have.

I appreciate myself. I give thanks for my wonderful life.

I am open to receive.

Everything I give to others is a gift to myself, as I give and I receive.

Every gift I give serves and empowers people.

Everything I give others honors and acknowledges their worth.

I give to myself generously.

I serve others to the best of my ability in all I say and do.

FOR FURTHER INFORMATION

If you have questions, a contribution, or a request for certain topics in the next edition of this book, please give us a call. We encourage your input to improve the effectiveness of this book as the leading reference on family financial planning through the understanding of the marriage relationship and through harnessing the power of team play to build substantial net worth. If you call us, we can assist you with your financial planning needs and questions.

If you would like to subscribe to our quarterly newsletter or tax newsletter, please give us a call. We would like to see all of you become "champion net worth builders."

For more information regarding Net Worth Building Seminars offered by Steven Pybrum, CPA & MBA, write to Post Office Box 23209, Santa Barbara, California 93121. Our telephone number is 805-962-1040.

Index

ORDER FORM

We encourage you to order copies for family members. Each husband-to-be and each wife-to-be should have a working copy of this book. Mark those pages that set forth the basis for your goals and priorities in reaching for a great relationship and a financially prosperous future.

Fax number: 805-421-4767

Telephone orders: 1-805-962-1040

Address for postal orders:
Abundance Publishing Company
Post Office Box 23209
Santa Barbara, CA 93121 USA
Web site: www.moneymarriageandcompatibility.com

Print your name and address (needed for all orders):
Name _____
Address _____
City _____ State _____ Zip _____
Telephone Number _____

Money and Marriage: Making It Work Together

_____ Quantity of books @ $17.95 _____
Sales tax for California orders @ 8.75% _____
Shipping & handling costs: $7.00 _____
Federal Express: $25.00 _____
TOTAL _____

Payment: _____ Check enclosed _____ Credit card

Type of card: ❑ Visa ❑ Mastercard

Name on card _____
Card number _____ Expires _____
Authorizing signature _____

_____ Would you like information on the next couples seminar?